Mother Mary Comes to Me
A Pop Culture Poetry Anthology

Karen Head & Collin Kelley
editors

MADVILLE
PUBLISHING

Lake Dallas, Texas

FIRST EDITION

Requests for permission to reprint or reuse material from this work should be sent to:

Permissions
Madville Publishing
PO Box 358
Lake Dallas, TX 75065

ACKNOWLEDGEMENTS

The editors gratefully acknowledge the publications, collections, and anthologies where these poems first appeared:

- *Ambushing Water* (Brick Road Poetry Press): "Lemon Breast of the Virgin Mary"
- *Annunciation: Sixteen Contemporary Poets Consider Mary* (Phoenicia Publishing): "Anointed"
- *Body and Soul* (Pirogue): "Welsh Pietà"
- *Cajun Mutt*: "St. Heresy in the Garden"
- *Cherry Tree* and *Our Lady of the Flood*: "Our Lady of 'No Regerts'"
- *Choice Words: Writers on Abortion* (Haymarket Books): "Hail Mary"
- *Cold Mountain Review*: "To the Girl Who Sees Miracles in Receding Water"
- *A Confusion of Marys* (Shearsman Books): "A Confusion of Marys"
- *Crab Creek Review*: "Mysteries of the Corn"
- *Dixmont* (Autumn House Press): "To All Those Who Prayed For Me"
- *Epoch*: "Annunciation"
- *Flycatcher*: "The Grace of Full Mary Hail"
- *Gorizia Notebook* (Finishing Line Press): "Santa Maria Sopra Minerva"
- *The Hour Between Dog and Wolf* (BOA Editions): "Plastic Beatitude"
- *Journey in the Crone* (Chuffed Buff Books): "Theokotos"
- *The MacGuffin*: "Encountering Mary Outside Lourdes"
- *Mass for Shut-Ins* (Backwaters Press): "An Agnostic Prays the Memorare"
- *Nimrod*: "Searching"
- *Pink Zinnia: Poems & Stories* (AuthorHouse): "A Lonely Six of Clubs"
- *Rhino*: "After a Stroke, My Mother Examines a Picture of the Icon of Our Lady of Guadalupe"
- *Slow To Burn* (MetroMania Press/Seven Kitchens Press): "The Virgin Mary Appears in a Highway Underpass"
- *Sonora Review*: "Formas Sagradas"
- *Writers of the Portuguese Diaspora in the United States and Canada: An Anthology* (Boavista Press): "The White City"
- *White Stag Journal*: "Statue Prayer at Fifteen"
- *The Women at the Well* (Portals Press/Stephen F. Austin University Press): "Mary: A Confession and Complaint"

Cover Design: Jacqueline Davis
Cover Image and Editor Photographs: Colin Potts

ISBN: 978-1-948692-42-7 paper, and 978-1-948692-43-4 ebook
Library of Congress Control Number: 2020941262

Contents

vii A Note from Editor Collin Kelley

viii A Note from Editor Karen Head

xiii Prologue
   Anonymous (translated by Richard Utz)
   I sing of a mayden

1. Ave Maria

   Ivy Alvarez
3 Anointed

   David-Matthew Barnes
5 Satellite

   Lee Ann Pingel
6 La Madonna de las Naranjas

   Larry D. Thacker
8 Thrift Store Gods

   Gustavo Hernandez
9 Formas Sagradas

   Jill Crammond
10 Mary Pays Homage

   Lara Gularte
12 The White City

   Linda Parsons
13 How Soft the Earth

   Laure-Anne Bosselaar
14 Plastic Beatitude

   Trebor Healey
15 Black Madonna

   Chelsea Clarey
17 Fear Not

   Cassondra Windwalker
19 We Are All Mary

   Lincoln Jaques
20 Our Gospa

2. I Am Woman

Grace Bauer
23   Mary: A Confession and Complaint

Jericho Brown
24   Nativity

Pablo Miguel Martínez
25   Adiós, o virgen de Guadalupe—

Janna Schledorn
27   Upon Realizing the Absence of Mothers

Ann Cefola
28   Theokotos

Catharine Clark-Sayles
29   Self Portrait as Annunciation

Tyson West
30   The Carpenter's Wife

Julie E. Bloemeke
32   Statue Prayer at Fifteen

Denise Duhamel and Maureen Seaton
34   Triptych

3. Along Comes Mary

JC Reilly
39   Stopping at a Starbucks in Egypt

Jennifer Martelli
40   Madonna Triptych, 1984

Mike James
42   Saint Heresy in the Garden

Franklin Abbott
43   A Lonely Six of Clubs

P.F. Anderson
47   Our Lady of Code

Robert Siek
48   Mutant Mary, Mother of Doom

Donna McLaughlin Schwender
50   Follow Me @HailSocialMary

Alison Pelegrin
51   Our Lady of 'No Regerts'

C. Cleo Creech
53   Mary Has Left the Building

4. Don't Stop Believin'

Rupert Loydell
57   A Confusion of Marys

Collin Kelley
58   The Virgin Mary Appears in a Highway Underpass

Karen Weyant
59   To the Girl Who Sees Miracles in Receding Water

Steven Reigns
60   A Stain in Florida

Robert Peake
61   The Virgin Mary Sits Across from Me, Applying Mascara on a Northbound London Tube

Karen Head
62   Encountering Mary Outside Lourdes

Fiona Pitt-Kethley
63   Ninja Virgin

Tina Kelley
65   Pareidolia, or "If It Makes Them Pray, That's OK"

Jennifer Clark
67   Searching

Blake Leland
68   Annunciation

Brent Calderwood
69   Mary's Confession

5. How Great Thou Art

Alice Friman
73   Mary at the Louvre Confronts Her Son

John C. Mannone
74   Sons

Jeannine Hall Gailey
76   Introduction in Indigo Children(After a Consult with a Medical Intuitive)

Robert E. Wood
77   Santa Maria Sopra Minerva

Julie Kane
79   Welsh Pietà

Lillo Way
80   From the *Winged Virgin of Quito,* "The Dancing Madonna," to Bernardo de Legarda, Wood Carver

Danielle Hanson
81 Lemon Breast of the Virgin Mary

Rupert Fike
82 Catholic Cemetery, Savannah

Megan Volpert
84 Giving Thanks at Seventy

6. Like a Prayer

Jane Varley
87 The Language of Prayer

Todd Robinson
88 An Agnostic Prays the *Memorare*

Deborah Hauser
89 Hail Mary

Marissa McNamara
90 The Grace of Full Mary Hail

Marcene Gandolfo
91 Fire is an Event, Not a Thing

Janet Lowery
92 Statue of Mary

Michelle Castleberry
94 To My Lady of the Three Oaks

Rick Campbell
96 To All Those Who Prayed for Me

Tom Daley
98 After a Stroke, My Mother Examines a Picture of the Icon of Our Lady of Guadalupe

Kyle Potvin
100 Mysteries of the Corn

102 Contributor Biographies
112 Editor Biographies

A Note from Editor Collin Kelley

Credit where credit is due: my co-editor Karen Head suggested the idea for this anthology seven years ago. We shopped the concept around to various presses, but there seemed to be a nervousness or hesitation about publishing a collection of poetry that doesn't deify Mary in a traditional way. As you'll see, a majority of these poems take the popular culture theme of this anthology to its farthest reaches. But whether it's sacred or profane, there is an undeniable passion in these poems and their genesis is the ever-mysterious Virgin Mary. Kudos then to Kim Davis and Madville Publishing for taking a leap of faith in presenting a vision of the Virgin that explores her persona and influence beyond the church.

My poem "The Virgin Mary Appears in a Highway Underpass," was Karen's introduction to my work when we met more than a decade ago. She wrote her Mary poem after visiting Lourdes, but I'll let her tell you that story. We were both fascinated by the ongoing sightings of Mary, whether it be a weeping statue, condensation on a Florida office building, in a field outside a small Georgia town, or ditchwater runoff inside a freeway tunnel. The faithful and media appear without fail, because Mary is still a headline-grabber and a source of art and inspiration. She remains a palimpsest, a metaphor, a prism to explore and reflect inner and outer conflicts, hopes, and desires on the small and large scale. Mary's virtue has remained intact and so has her inscrutability, for which we have only the source material to blame, but that has allowed artists to remix, reinterpret, and reexamine her motives and faith through the millennia.

We received hundreds of poems for this anthology and, I think I can speak for Karen on this as well, choosing this final selection was one of the toughest choices we've ever had to make. There are poets here that will be familiar to you and poets we can't wait for you to discover, but what they all have in common is that the Virgin Mary lingers no matter their faith or belief. Perhaps in reading these fantastic poems, you'll get closer to unravelling the truth, or at least find some divine inspiration of your own.

A Note from Editor Karen Head

As Collin mentioned, the idea of this anthology has been years in the making, and, yes, as poets we trace our first interactions to Collin's poem "The Virgin Mary Appears in a Highway Underpass"—coincidently, a poem I first heard him read at an event held in a small art space on the lowest level of the building I moved into fifteen years later. Mary has her hands in many things—real estate among them. My own poem for this collection, "Encountering Mary Outside Lourdes" reflects both on Lourdes, perhaps the place in the world most associated with Mary's appearances, and on the idea of Mary appearing where and when she is needed; my (re)vision being one that offers her as a contemporary figure trying to communicate beyond language.

Collin and I also share a love for Paris, and when we were watching Notre-Dame in flames, we turned back to this project with renewed passion. While it was wonderful to see how people were pledging billions of Euros to restore Notre-Dame, thoughts of churches razed by arson much closer to home came in to sharp view. Collin and I, both of us born in Georgia, are also intensely aware of the violence that has been committed against Black communities and their churches. Could Mary inspire some philanthropy on that front? We wanted to find out, and Madville was on-board with that mission. Our profits from this collection will be donated to restoration efforts for burned-out Black churches in the Southern United States.

There's Something about Mary: About the Sections

What is it about Mary that inspires poetry from the religious to the secular? Despite her place in Christian theology, most strongly seen in the Roman Catholic faith, Mary transcends those Biblical boundaries and is a central figure in popular culture. Our prologue poem, the 15th C. Middle English lyric, celebrates the Annunciation (the most common title and reference we saw in the hundreds of submissions we reviewed for this collection). However, scholars have argued that the poem was likely well known by the

15th c. and may date back to the 13th c. The lyric begins with a declaration of song, and would likely have been sung. Certainly, the rhythms and rhymes in the original Middle English would lend themselves to song. For example, here is the second stanza in the original text:

> he came also stylle
> þer his moder was
> as dew in aprylle,
> þat fallyt on þe gras.

Even if your Middle English is a bit rusty (ours is!), you can sound out the song-like qualities. We are indebted to Richard Utz for his translation which modernizes the English while maintaining the original lyric qualities.

This collection is divided into six sections that investigate Mary through a variety of themes through the eyes of contemporary poets. To elaborate those themes, we have chosen songs that are also broadly recognizable whether in religious or popular music.

Part One: Ave Maria

This section explores the theme of Mary as a traditional religious figure and as a mother. From Ivy Alvarez's stunning portrayal of the annunciation, in which Mary reflects, "God is a hum, a note I know / In my heart. Hungry and full." to Lincoln Jaques' sober contemplation of Mary appearing in pre-war Croatia, where we are promised, "One day you will arrive to a place / where She will know you, waiting / for as long as memory can recall." Mary is depicted still as carrying the weight of her motherhood, for Jesus and for everyone, in ways that are both traditional and immediate.

Part Two: I Am Woman

This section explores notions of Mary through a feminist perspective. Throughout this section, Mary demonstrates resistance. She is not quick to agree to her anointment, as Catharine Clark-Sayles describes: "The angel clears his throat, / ready to announce. Finger to my lips, I shake my head,"—Mary wants one last dance. Or, as Jericho Brown considers, what if Mary wanted to escape her identity? The poems in this section explore how Mary, if able to self-determine her fate, might have chosen a different path.

Part Three: Along Comes Mary

The nascence of this collection is here, where the poems place Mary in popular culture contexts. Here are poems that consider Mary at Starbucks (JC Reilly) or how she might be viewed in the context of computer code (P.F. Anderson) or having her juxtaposed with Ruth Bader Ginsberg and Anthony Bourdain (C. Cleo Creech), among others that position Mary firmly in a 21st century context.

Part Four: Don't Stop Believin'

From Lourdes to modern day underpasses, Mary continues to "appear" in a variety of ways and people look for comfort by finding her in everyday experiences and places. Along with the catalyst poems by the editors, this section includes poems that reflect on Mary appearances, whether in the traditional religious sense or in more unexpected (and even cinematic) ways, like Fiona Pitt-Kethley's version of Mary as a nighttime ninja superhero.

Part Five: How Great Thou Art

Ekphrastic poetry, that is poetry about other artworks, lends itself particularly well to the story of Mary. Few figures have been portrayed in art more than Mary has. From Kane's traditional consideration in "Welsh Pietà" to Megan Volpert's Long Island sing-along, Mary as a foundational element in a variety of genres is key to understanding her prevalence in both religious and secular culture.

Part Six: Like a Prayer

Finally, this section explores how Mary continues to be a point of invocation, a point of hope. "Hail Mary…pray for us, now and in the hour of our death." The final section elaborates the need of humans to believe in something bigger than themselves, and Mary as intercessor is another way that her legacy transcends boundaries; this is even true for Todd Robinson's agnostic speaker in "Mary knows." Kyle Potvin leaves us with prayers to Mary for, among other petitions, "the teen shot near the corner." Ultimately the final lines of the anthology leave readers with a subtle but devasting shift to second person:

> After all, an ear to the ground is useless.
> You know what's coming.

Not unlike the famous William Stafford poem, "Traveling through the Dark"—we are forced to consider how the "you" invoked is Mary, yes, but also each one of us.

Prologue

I syng of a mayden

Anonymous, 15 C.
Translated by Richard Utz

I sing of a maiden
Matchless is she.
King of Kings she chose
For her son to be.

He came as still
Where his mother was
As dew in April
That descends on the grass.

He came as still
To his mother's bower
As dew in April
That descends on the flower.

He came as still
Where his mother lay
As dew in April
That descends on the hay.

Mother and maiden
There's never been another.
Well may such a lady
Be God's mother.

1. Ave Maria

Anointed

i

It would be as if I had been praying all my life
Becoming a woman at the same time
Forgiving everyone, and in continuance
I've only just met my husband
Already betrothed, though still to be wed
His face is kind and we are young

ii

God is a hum, a note I know
In my heart. Hungry and full.

I am simultaneous
All the time.

The kitchen tiles, the pleasant table
At the centre an empty fruit bowl

Which then? The bird or the sound of it
Dull on the glass? Two steps
Toward the balcony there
It lies stunned on its back
Beak opens then shuts
Claws in reflexive grip
I look at the mark it left outside
A wingbeat on the window soft etched
Oils from its feathers traced
A bird in profile

On the balcony the bird is gone

iii

Perfumed
A sudden gift
In the fruit bowl, a yellow plum
Ripening and perfect even then

Satellite

Mary, where were you when the moon split
in two? Were you on the outskirts of town—
your back pressed to the holy ground, face up,
confusing stars for comets but still wishing?

You heard salvation before you spoke it, the rumble
roaring down, slicing the fronds: what a rush. Leaves
you to tremble in the quake of your youth until
your virginal mind becomes hot and wild. Pure.

They reach for you. Yet, you'd rather capture
the lunar swirls, hold the shattered moon, tender
satellite in your praying hands. Somewhere,
the tide is also broken and weeping. Listen.

Joseph's been dreaming again. They want to kill
your son. They want you to appear every time
they need a miracle. You hear the constant
desperation of faceless sinners: the haunting echo

of their hungry howls. Calling.

La Madonna de las Naranjas

It is Christmas Eve in the desert.
Not the desert of Palestine or Egypt
or even the desert of my heart,
though it is one.
This is the desert of privilege and poverty,
playground and prison.
By which I mean if your name is Jimenez
or Torres or Ramos, you are going nowhere
unless it's to *México* when your cousin who works
lawns has enough money for gas.
By which I mean if your name is Myers
or Johnson or White, you live behind
ramparts and gates fifteen feet high,
and if you are going somewhere
it is to Jackson Hole for the summer
or maybe to Gelson's market for *marrons glacés*
or maybe, just maybe, to church,
like me, driving past miles of walls,
some softened with oleander or palms,
some softened with orange trees,
heavy with midwinter fruit
no one but the grackles will harvest.

Nothing will grow in the hot sand
of my self. I cannot find the Madonna
in this church that projects prayers
on a screen above the altar,
clip art of the Christ child
smiling down at the crêche.
Where could she be? Where *would*
she be, a brown-skinned girl,
a migrant, going to put her name
on a register?

Among the oranges, of course.
Hiding in the small strip of green
between cinderblock and asphalt,
the only space here that is fruitful.

Thrift Store Gods

She stood tall and lean, holding her son on her hip,
well above lesser examples of *Madonna and Child*,

their glazed ceramic sheen calling out to someone, me,
under the friendly, jittery Salvation Army florescence,

upon inspection of the bottom rim, a hand-made gift
From Beanie, To Mom, 1974, in a teenager's cursive.

Over forty years old, it was feeling relic-like by now.
Inside its hollowness, halfway down, is stuffed tissue.

When I noticed it and used a knife to gently pry it out,
I joked, *Wouldn't it be strange to find some money?*

And there it was. A dollar. Or, half a dollar, at least,
pressed down into the statue, awaiting my amazement:

ragged, soiled, torn roughly between George's eyes,
a tiny signature, a first name, *Romana*, the legible hint

as to the age of the bill. *Romana Acosta Banuelos—*
she was US Treasurer, appointed by Nixon in 1971.

She served until 1974. Could this bill have been new
when it was shoved into the statue back in 1974? Or

just an aging scrap bill secreted into the icon for luck
in any year since? The other half anywhere, nowhere?

Did *Madonna and Child* mind the baggage so long,
holding something within, a message for the curious.

And should I head back to that West Virginia store,
leave a mysterious fifty-cent piece behind. Call it even.

Formas Sagradas

To a child the Virgenes return mechanized
over the pitayas in the countryside. Night masses
of steel braids and copper manteaus over Atotonilco
and its ruby wealth, breathing dahlia blossoms
from the vents in their joints, magnetized segments
hovering warm sighs away from each other. Circles

of stars around their fingers raised in benediction,
these ticking-brass mothers leak milk, bake bread
keep watch over and irrigate the guasana fields.
Bone white face panels shift—crescent, bullhorn
new to full—to illuminate the way for children
herding cattle. How these whirring monoliths

return us to the old way—synthesized blessings
over the hands of old men offering papayas
and mangos *de los de antes.* To a child, these
mothers are the black mist of manufactured
thunderclouds purifying veins, disarming men.
Healing the grief of widows and the childless.

How their knees slowly trail down the illuminated
walkways of their temples. Paying back mandas:
the sick injected to health, the work remunerated,
the land kept. Crying children convincing their
reluctant parents to enter, to not ever feel afraid.
These mothers are the same as ever. Call to them.

Mary Pays Homage

The art of mothering isn't hard to master;
so many children filled with the intent
to be lost that their loss is no disaster.

So much depends
upon

a booster
seat

sitting on the roof
of an SUV

while a wrong-shoes-for-the-weather
mother

searches
for her keys and morning coffee.

When I say children, I mean
gingerbread house,
mean step-mother,
mean

artificial slate sidewalk
artfully arranged,
leading
to a front door with a wreath,
a witch inside making dinner.

Lose your family every day. Accept the fluster
of slamming doors, the mealtime badly spent.

Stand etherized before the crusted sink,
your hair a half-deserted streak behind you

while the children come and go
talking (each one) of the one that got away.

After the second glass of wine
you will know
what it is you plan to do
with your one wild and precious life.

After a fashion, the chickens will raise themselves,
will have sense enough
to come in out of the rain.

The White City

Above seven hills the sol star shines,
casts away shadow.
Wind carries time around, and past,
raises up dust.

When white Freesia leans
against stained glass,
the fadista sweeps heat
down the boulevards.

A glow seizes albescent patinas,
as specters buff the domed church,
and ethers rise up with fish-eyes.

The Tagus River brings home the lost ones
through wrack, and conch,
messages of salt.

On the Avenida da Liberdade,
people call out for Santo Antonio,
discover lost things.

Find the Madonna down a quiet alley.
She stands on a gate,
uses aquamarines to cut the air,
then hems the sky with gold thread.

How Soft the Earth

How soft the earth is here, grounds
of the Loretto Motherhouse, as if every
inch is tilled for planting, honeycombed
with openheartedness—the nuns dying
out, wedded as much to red-winged
blackbirds in the sycamores as to
the Bridegroom. Our softness,
for my own defenses are crumbling,

is more than spring breaking out,
slate yielding to apple green, more
than the shock of life sifted to meal,
the cross of ash thumbed on foreheads.
Dirt gives way, yet holds me in alignment,
the Winter Worm Moon low and huge
over the Mary and Joseph lakes,
closer and closer to how earth
receives our mystery.

Plastic Beatitude

     Our neighbors, the Pazzotti's, live in a narrow
canary-yellow house with their two daughters & husbands,
five kids, Mrs. Pazzotti's old father, a tortoise shell cat
& a deaf poodle. Their yard is my childhood dream:
     toys, bikes, tubs, chimes, 3 BBQs, & garden
sculptures: Mickey Mouse on one leg, two turquoise
toads in a love seat under a polka-dotted parasol
& St. Joseph carrying a lantern—his other
     blessing hand broken at the wrist.
On the pink and green deck railing a pinwheel
procession thrashes the air with each breeze
like clumsy angels nailed to their destiny.
     At the end of that yard, two electric chords
shoot up to the garage's roof. One chord connects to a big
blue neon insect-electrocuter, and the other snakes to,
then slips into a pedestal cemented on the cornice.
     And there she stands, in plastic beatitude,
and six feet of it, the Madonna in her white robe
& blue cape, arms outstretched, lit from within
day & night, blessing the Pazzotti's,
     their yard & neighbors, calling the Lord's
little insects to her shining light, before sending them
straight to the zapper & frying those little heretics
drawn by a last temptation.

Black Madonna

All the dark mountains are her
and she sits within them
as if within a shawl of snow, of stone
Our Lady of the Dark Blood

Menstruating volcano
I get used to the heat of this molten flow
I get used to it like hot water scalding
And let it burn me
Her companionship is a sweatlodge
and I let myself burn and soften like a squash

I'm a blackened potato
and pain is more about time
more about acceptance
which too is about time
than suffering

Time is a crooked old man
she drives away with stones

And I am more about night
more about confusion
more about blindness and surrender
more about black smoke
and choking
more about a black hole than a star
And she's told me they are the same

And when I awake in the middle of the night
her body before me
the sacred mountain
I see the rage of her tenderness

The nightsky is a charred forest fire of starlight
burning embers

Oh dark mother
you press wisdom into us like clay
we are the weakest kind of stone

Fear Not

I imagine she thirsted for leavening,
Knew the Passover as the famine
And welcomed eagerly the risen loaf.
I imagine she saw it make more of itself
       Air-hunger
Help it make something of nothing.

I imagine she did not fear the lamb's blood
Even when small
(Though they thought she did, and comforted her)
But she stood in a gory portal
And felt something deep
Deep.

I imagine she spiced the lamb with a deft hand
Making mere leaf and flesh into
Something.

She was told, not asked.
I don't need to imagine this.
As her belly rises like a loaf
With the shortening days
They praise her loudly, louder still,
among crystal and banner and organpipe
For *Let it be as you have said.*

Yet I praise her silently
For *Let it be as you shall choose.*

I imagine he was asked.
I imagine she made something out of the nothing
       a question
       a confession
       a proposal of her own

To make the choice his own.
To safeguard his faith with her own.
To make their marriage their own.

I imagine she began as she meant to go on;
Hungry to hope,
Ravenous to provide,
Throwing her own body in the way
(the child of her body in the way)
Of the lashing-down of choice.

We Are All Mary

it's hard to watch the mother at the manger
and not grieve for her, hard to carry joy
past the open door of horror and not linger
in its frame, transfixed by cruelty
and its regular, common price—but every mother
knows that door is there, and life forbids
we bar its way, block its passage
in any way: we do our best
to keep those little feet far
from that awful room, but the price of creation
is steep, and each breath is resignation
to that cost: a laughing burst of speed,
a heedless glance behind, and the precious one
may stumble out of reach—some willfully
charge into that darkness, and others still
are snatched without a warning
by cold miasmic winds that gust, unchecked,
through that hideous, watchful, gaping door:

somewhere there are mothers
untouched by that cold wind,
somewhere there are children whose feet
never venture across that threshold,
but I have forgotten them all,
and in swaddling blankets and the blood of birth,
I see only graveclothes and the stains of inhumanity.

Our Gospa

On account of a pilgrimage
to a place I knew nothing about,
we turned up in Medjugorje; a day
scorched by sun, candles ablaze
like a forest on fire.
Heads bowed to the earth.

They first saw the apparition in 1981;
later the war came too—that was no
apparition. The way they described Her
makes me think of a glazed doll, the
type you can buy for 100 kuna.

The vision will carry you across deserts
or hold you paralyzed. Let me count
the days when She weeps, allow the
jealous priests to scorn, allow the softened
edges of the sun to spin, like they describe.
Wait for the silence to take over.

One day you will arrive to a place
where She will know you, waiting
for as long as memory can recall.

*   Gospa = Lit. 'Lady' (Croat), in reference to Mother Mary, who has allegedly periodically appeared to a group of children since 1981 in Medjugorje.

2. I Am Woman

Mary: A Confession and Complaint

Legend shows me acquiescent.
Don't believe a word. I would have ignored
that angel if I could have, but he made me
an offer I couldn't refuse.
Even now I blame my failing vision
on those few moments of terrifying light.

I was not an ambitious girl.
I loved Joseph and looked forward
to our marriage and children who would grow,
and in their time, have children.
Our days, I assumed, would be simple.
Joseph in his shop. Me in my kitchen.
At night we'd share the better moments.
I would shine beneath his
hands like polished wood.

It wasn't fair to ask me to bear all that
pain without ever knowing pleasure.
And if I could have only one child,
I would have much preferred a girl.
My son, though I know he loved us,
was never affectionate. He moved
as if his body were not his own.
He had a cold, distant look in his eyes.

And Joseph, though he was always kind
and never doubted me, could not get close
to the boy. He grew more silent
with the years, more sullen.
And I could never bring myself to say
forget about the angel! Or to confess
the desire he might have found in me
if he had dared to look
beyond the piety, beneath the veils.

Nativity

I was Mary once.
Somebody big as a beginning
Gave me trouble
I was too young to carry, so I ran
Off with a man who claimed not
To care. Each year,
Come trouble's birthday,
I think of every gift people get
They don't use. Oh, and I
Pray. Lord, let even me
And what the saints say is sin within
My blood, which certainly shall see
Death—see to it I mean—
Let that sting
Last and be transfigured.

Adiós, o virgen de Guadalupe—

a wave, a wail, an endless loop
of hymn, of delirium. We laud her,
this brown-skinned girl, nimble,

balanced on a slip of moon,
headstrong as only mujercitas
her age can be, urge her back

to her celestial jefe. Go back
where you're safe, chula.
What are you doing here,

among the nopales and the men
who'll take ugly advantage?
Your heavenly Pops will fret.

Why can't you be more like that
immaculate girl who dresses
in creamy white and sky blue? he'll cry.

No seas tan exigente, asking ese indio
humilde to build you a shrine,
as if picking out a shiny trinket,

demanding a sign of his devotion,
as if conjuring roses in winter
were nothing, just like that. Don't be

quick to part your cloak for any güey,
dropping a field of stars on which to lie
for your heated entwining. You are always

with us, morenita, in spiky sun rays,
your outline in handprints when your raza
is pressed against walls, against our wills.

Adiós, mi reina. Go find what you seek
en el otro lado. Here we will wait and hope
and pray, but for now, ¡Adiós, adiós!

Upon Realizing the Absence of Mothers

Searched for her in ruffled hibiscus
and fallen nests
(she weeding rows of day lilies)

Searched for her on warm shores
in sand piper threads
(she skipping in mountain streams)

Looked in prayer books and bibles
(saw father in heaven, son on cross,
ghost, dove descending)

Searched for her in canopy of trees
along afternoon path
(she calling, a call I could not catalog)

Oh, walk with me again,
walk with me and help me
name wild birds

Theokotos

*A Greek term coined by the early church for the Virgin meaning
"God-bearer"*

Some women want to abandon their independence.
They desire the roundness of a pear,
the mutuality of seed in flower.
They long for their bodies to become a home.

They chase the angel of annunciation.

Those souls who then appear inside,
microscopic, grow fickle:
they inhale liquid waste and wonder.
Bumping against soft organs, they panic.

Some beings, the Buddhist explains, *like to practice incarnating.*

Like rude house guests, they depart untidily—
with a wrench of red bubbles,
or having endure the terrible tunnel to light,
vacate their eyes and abandon their curled blue form.

There are lessons that must be learned, says the therapist.

She would never meet the son she in jest called *Senator.*
Another pushed out a dwarf and, for a few hours,
sang lullabies to his misshapen head. Other burials take place
in the bathroom, where women on knees gaze at bright tile.

I am poured out like water.

The garden locked in flowers:
Divinity, come through this flesh door,
leave your paradise now
or risk destroying ours.

Self Portrait as Annunciation

Incarnadine: sun seen through eyelids closed against delicious heat,
vessels traced in black against the glow, a sleepy drowsing buzz—
my thoughts, like lazy flowers scattering dust, consider the day and chores,

slide near the edge of conscious to the place where UFOs pair
with missing socks and rains of frogs, where odd ideas slip into dreams,

so that I stand before a jukebox coined with diamonds to play
exactly whatever song is needed now. Music keyed in scent:
a jazzy eucalyptus, a ballad played in rosemary, notes of lemon *lieder.*

I slip a used-up wedding ring into the slot and get a musky tune
played slow and low—for dancing solo and when the angel

taps for cutting in, I smile and dance away. The angel clears his throat,
ready to announce. Finger to my lips, I shake my head,
dance back into my body pinking in the sun, watch shadows flick

beneath my lids, content to stretch into the ordered thud of blood
moving under skin from lips to hips to toes.

The Carpenter's Wife
December, 2019

She was not a woman you noticed right away—
not like my dead Judith whose loud laughter and footsteps still echo off
      the walls of our home
when I close my eyes,
a house our youngest daughter now keeps with her own testament of order.
Our foods swims not so spicily cooked in the same limestone vessels
      nor does
my clothing lie folded as comfortably as it had been caressed in Judith's
      strong hands.
Yet I dare not complain to Sarah for if she left for some young man's
      arms and lies
no one would sweep my dust and clean my plates.
I keep stitching broken sandals and crafting new with a jibe or joke
for those who trade with me like Joseph and his wife Mary.
The first few times she stopped
I could sense her skill with needles—her cloak and tunic well-formed—
I would later learn the intricacy of her stitching admiring her work
as she lay naked next to me.
Of course, she was the one who teased me first
batting her eyes as she drew out my story in the banter of our trading.
She too first touched my forearm.
Unsure of the shade of her desire I hesitated
still my starving for a woman's hand pulling me close made me
drop to the magic of time's syrup crystalizing into diamonds of now.
Her husband and son had left to craft walls for the tanner's house
and she had seen my daughter leave for the marketplace,
she swept into my shop on our first visitation
and at the look in those hard brown eyes
I put up the closed sign
then she and I both broke the silence of my chambers.
In the distance a donkey brayed
and the weaver's woman across the wadi yelled at her husband—
my tongue hunted for the sweetness in the dark forest of her triangle

while she found a way to fold my manhood into her being.
So we continued in stolen moments never fearing the punishment of
      adulteress
for as she laughingly preached to me
"It be a sin only if the points and sighs of our passion alter God's design."
She would have made a wondrous wife for she loved the same spices as I
but she kept whispering of her son's destiny and hers when he left town
      at thirty
to preach to strangers annoying the Romans,
who I confess, have been far better governors than our Pharisees.
It takes only a few coins to purchase their disinterest.
I warned my loving milf of the dangers her son faced tugging
on the priests' fine cloaks.
Then as suddenly as our intimacy flared
she abruptly rose to follow her son on his strange sojourn.
I am sure that Joseph and my daughter
never suspected when the moonlight cuts the desert air
like a scimitar into my sleeping quarters where I lie alone
I miss my fingers' last caress of Judith's soft inner thigh
with as much sorrow as my loss of Mary's tight body and skillful hands.
She never returned to me after the terrible end her son met at Jerusalem
and the theft of his corpse a few days later.

Statue Prayer at Fifteen

Mother, in my world,
virginity is defined
by loss.

Admission: an easy
litmus. As soon as I open
to confession, their touches
turn from want to sister.

But here I am on my knees, still
in this jaded light, your static mouth
jeweled in the cut of votive flame.

What if I believe this
is my way? That for once
I have found the diadem of *no*
as a kind of salvation, at last

a place where I am heard?
What if I think of your face
smiling in *yes?* When I whisper
in the thresh of desire, what if I pray
to hold, wait for the one true found?

I cannot bear their eager lips,
their breath heavy at the chapel
of want, the way they try their hands
at the altar of my legs. I soften
to their kisses, yes, the rare
sweetness of their words when
they are without motive.

Someone has painted a heart
on your hand. Someone has

touched you with gold. I tip
my forehead to your cracked hem,
hardened in its line. My knees grow numb
with leaning. I whisper up to you:

Oh Mary. Oh marry. Oh merry.
Is it all a trinity of trickery, a prayer
of persuasion, of false faith?

And still the problem
of this star, crossed
over my body, forever
this burden we call light.

Triptych

For Stacey Waite and Brandon Som

Mary tried to fight off the Angel (#MaryToo),
her womb full of snow, sky, and bickering clouds.
She thrust her thumb into an orange peel and pulled
just as the newly-named Lady Gaga constellation appeared.
Mary recalled her own immaculate, bloodless birth
aboard a commuter train etching its way down the Hudson
as Ethan Hawk told Julie Delpy they have "a connection"
in Vienna and my father donned his old Navy uniform
for my dying mom. Oh virginity, where have you gone?
Everyone's gaga over blue now, Virgin Airlines, Pure-e
Energy Drinks. *I'm sorry! Come back! I'll do anything
not to climb another apple tree. I've already climbed six!*
Lady Gaga's Aunt Joanne died at nineteen after a sexual assault.
Some say the Mother of God died trying to save her.

Mary's death is a rumor, a poem, a hoax. She whistles
like green parrots and scrub jays in fishtail palms
beside an orange grove you can smell in Maine. Rip that skin
off your knee as you topple from your custom Eminem skateboard
and you'll be glad you were born posing with angels
who'd pulled you (the train) from your mother's tunnel.
(Any movie with a train scene makes me weep.)
Cry now—you'll pee less later
is what my Aunt Mary said right before she died of heartbreak,
a bowl of peanut M&M's on her nightstand,
all the nieces singing "Stay Awake" from *Mary Poppins*.
I never climbed a tree and now it seems too late to try.
So I fill my cheeks with M&M's and munch myself to sleep
and dream Mother Mary hosts her own Supper, no one to betray her.

Mary was a great cook and party planner. She drove her old
Honda filled with goodies all over the mountains and lanes,
headed to her kitchen to make her famous orange peel chicken

with Julia Child, patron saint of French cuisine
who was born long and lean, "a basketball player" joked the doc
of divinity who'd been trained in male bonding and cant,
as Eric Idle, on a cross, sang "Always Look On the Bright Side of Life."
Mary—wife, mother, kitchen goddess—agreed religiously
as she looked for her lost pearl earring asking St. Jude for help
(he a distant cousin of her fatally famous child).
Why don't you stay? I have some gingerbread in the oven,
Mary would say to tree huggers & social climbers alike
whose mortal children ran toward the delicious smell
as Mary coldcocked Gabriel and opened her arms.

3. Along Comes Mary

Stopping at a Starbucks in Egypt

Mary lifts her feet to the stool beside her,
swollen like little Glad-bags filled with water,
as Joe hands her a decaf latte, extra foam.

He sits down, sips his two shots of espresso,
and says, *How are you holding up?*
He looks at her belly, shakes his head. Not long now.

Oh, you know how it is, says Mary. *He's kicking
and it's a long way to Bethlehem.*
She chugs down her latte, detonates a belch.

Joe winces. *Sorry hon,* she says, grinning.
She's been like this ever since that guy
with the wings. Joe's dad had warned him:

Son, he said, *when your Mom was round yon
with you, all she wanted was wine and gyros
with extra peanut butter, and she farted enough*

*to start the hole in the ozone layer. That's the way
with women. Once they got matzos in the over,
their manners go straight to Gehenna.*

So far his wife hadn't been as bad as that, but Joe
stayed in the shop as much as possible, building
shelves for sale and a cradle in his spare time.

Hey babe, Mary wheedles, *get me another?
I'd get it myself but . . .*
Joe slouches back to the counter, buys her a grande,

another quarter bushel of wheat he won't see again.
When he gives her the drink, he expels a sigh.
So much work for someone else's prodigy.

Madonna Triptych, 1984

I.

My heart beat boom boom boom
when I stole things from my parents' room:

tortoiseshell cup, the rosaries I grabbed in my fist—
some tarnished, one with a bone crucifix.

On the bureau, the triptych mirror refracted light
from the windows with ivory drapes and blinds.

The stone Madonna wore my favorite strand:
the pearl rosary moons on a tarnished chain.

I held five decades of luminescent spit
and mother of pearl to my breast, my lips,

fingered the beads, all sweaty & tangled—
my ribcage felt corseted laced up and bridled.

No one ever missed a single thing
or heard me leave—I think

II.

even in my dreams I fear no one
will ever hear me. Last night I tugged

a steel knife from an old wound, diseased—
the long cool blade pulled easily

from a cloudy sky: the sky at night
refracting the pearl milk moon full and fat.

On my pine bureau, the tortoiseshell cup
holds the pearl and blonde wood beads, dust

clogs their chains, dust sprinkles down
like starlight through the open windows,

and because this is my dream, the knife
became a black and silver corded mic

I held to my breast, my lips.
The long cord wrapped around me, my ribs—

III.

and because this is my dream, the mic
belonged to Madonna crawling in white

across the dusty stage in tulle and lace,
corseted a bride like a virgin her necklaces—

three strands of pearls, rhinestones for refraction.
A fat rosary with globe decades tightened

around her neck: the choker gleamed,
echoed her silver boytoy belt, and still she

was singing, *oooh you make me feel ooooh
yeah you make me feel shiny and new—*

all laced up in whale bone or plastic stays
ribcaged Madonna got down girl-cow low,

dragged that crucifix across the wood. It loomed
over the waxy shine, bounced to the bass beat boom.

Saint Heresy in the Garden

Little comes to me as quickly as I wish. There's always that.
I treat my hang ups, phobias, and failings as my most vital parts.

One habit is calling everyone Mary if I like them well enough.
In that case, the name is a gift. Some respond by giving back a quiz.

Some friends part from me. Maybe tired from my latest hobby.
Exhausted from certain ticks… my propensity to use a ball cap to catch rain.

Any wisdom I have comes from looking, on an almost monthly basis, at
Gas station calendars, black-and-white movies, and discarded Beatle lyrics.

It's not always enough to believe in darkness or the simple broken-hearted.
So I believe in Bigfoot, jackalopes, and Mother Mary illuminated on
        burnt toast.

A Lonely Six of Clubs

Homage to Gypsy Ricker
translater / tramsmitter

a lonely six of clubs
stuck in a chain link fence
edging a motel parking lot
just outside of Birmingham
taken months later
to Mother Mary
of the red hand
who always lives on the outskirts
just shy of the fork in the road
she lives behind the room
she works in
you can smell her lunch
and barely hear a radio
and maybe an old person coughing
through the wall
richly decorated with religious images
mostly catholic but eclectic
an illuminated sacred heart
at the center
hard to miss
underneath
peacock feathers
in a silver vase

she seems almost tired
when she opens the door
and welcomes you in
she tells you her price
(thirty dollars for fifteen minutes)
directs you to a hard chair opposite
where she sits comfortably
in a big overstuffed armchair
a wooden tray in front of her

a glass of water on it beside
a solid brass candlestick holder
she puts a white candle in
lights it with a match
she blows out with a puff
you smell sulfur sharp and brief
she closes her eyes for one deep breath
then opens them slowly
looks directly at you
and asks
how can I help?

I hand her the card
explain how I found it
she smiles and tells me
you make my job easy
she takes another breath
holding the card with fingers of both hands
in front of her heart
she looks down
inhales
looks up
and begins

are you afraid
of ghosts?
no, my voice dips
in disagreement
she smiles and says
that is always
the first question
she asks

she pauses as if in thought
more faint music from the other side
a faraway cough
she takes a sip of water
breathes deeply and resumes

this time as she exhales
the flame of the candle
flares and flickers
do strange people
seek you out
she inquires
what do you mean
by strange I reply
good she says
then nods her head
her eyelids droop
her breathing changes
time passes
she snorts twice
and raises her head, hesitates
I hear what sounds like
birds singing outside the window
then her voice
when swallows build
you will begin as well
begin what
I mutter

she takes another sip
and another long pause
and then begins
I see a body of water
still water
she seems distracted
do I hear a toilet flush?
its time to stop now
she says adding quietly
all will be well
then blows out the candle

as she sees me to the door
holding the ten and the twenty
I just gave her

she touches my arm lightly
with her other hand
one question for you
she says
if you don't mind
I nod
why were you there?
why were you
in Birmingham?
for my grandmother's funeral
I confess
she looks at me
like I'm a child
sweet she says
she gave you
one more clue
a kiss good-bye
I sigh
deflated
by grief
but I do not cry

oh she says
abruptly
as if something
had just
occurred to her
buy yourself a music box
one with a dancer
under a globe
then she catches my eyes
with hers
and no matter what
anybody tells you
there is never
a last chance

Our Lady of Code

Bits and bytes swirl, she streams
zeroes and ones into
iterative layers
of meaning, she stacks her
hexadecimal in
building blocks and walls, she
carves code into paintings
and poems punctuated
with slashes, pipes, and points.
She is delicate and
terse. She has a tiny
footprint. Her hands are base
ten embodied.
Her eyes are binary
and beautiful. Her heart
is Boolean, her heart
is fuzzy, her heart is
false and true. Her desires
are nested, and spoon like
parentheses; hungers
feed forward, and if you
cannot forgive, let go.
Her dreams process if-then
statements knotted inside
for-loops. They are visions,
they are visionary,
they are her afterthoughts
compounded. They could be
almost infinite (ebb
and sea, flood and fill, loop)
except that she wakes in
a break. [Pause.] Here, she says,
adjust the bounds, like this.

Mutant Mary, Mother of Doom

Virgin Mary statues rebranded by John Waters's *Pecker*.
Her magic and creep factor lost to a hand over mouth,
an attempt to hide laughter, anticipating her saying,
"Full of Grace," like a puppet version did in multiple scenes.
I want to shout, "Beg your pardon," and kneel in front of her,
remind her how her son haunted me as a child, showed up
in nightmares knocking at windows dressed like Doctor Doom
from Marvel Comics. And maybe she was there too, all cosplay
as the mutant villain Destiny, dressed in a powder blue bodysuit,
thigh-high boots, and cape connected to a swab-shaped helmet—
a yellow face drawn as moving death mask or was that her skin.
Well I know she had the power of precognition, was blind,
and often fought the X-Men. Mary, mother of God,
were you crouched behind the roses, unaware your layers
of fabric made enemies of thorns, like hey you've seen
the worst of them, punctures on your son's forehead and scalp.
And I want to try saying a Hail Mary but know you're listening,
hold your hands extending from your quarter-capsule
amphitheater, zone out on its sky blue interior
like we watch you float in the Caribbean,
beachside but calm waters, what I imagine
your son walking on but hidden inside
a green hooded cape, sneaking up
on the Invisible Woman, like knock
knock, I see you. Open the damn door.
Worship me in your sleep. He told me
his mother didn't raise a dummy. His iron
mask clicks against glass—every window
on the first floor of one-seventeen Burns Ave.
Five-year-old me tries to hide behind a space heater;
somehow it's never warm enough in the room I end up in.
So no way am I spellbound or foretelling another lifetime
downhill, whether I ever believe again, me in the suit
I wore to my communion when I was in second grade.

It's now time to pretend to pray. I decide to bearhug
a stiff Virgin Mary, lawn ornament blessing flowers,
the ones she shades at certain hours, and I beg her
to speak, to clearly say, "Full of Grace," sensing
her hips and upper arms crumbling. Just say,
"Full of Grace." Goddamn it. Let me know
I didn't fear your family for nothing.

Follow Me @HailSocialMary

Zuckerberg doesn't know it yet,
but social media isn't just for mortals.
Father frowns when I talk about
how amazing it would have been
if I could have Instagrammed the Last Supper
or live-tweeted my Assumption,
but he agrees it's never too late
to reconnect with old friends
or to make new ones.
Selfies and Skyping are out,
but I'll gladly accept your Facebook friend request.
Secret prayer request?
WhatsApp message me at Vir-gin-Mary (847-446-6279).
Just feel like chatting?
Text me anytime.
Seriously.
A.N.Y.T.I.M.E.
Until then,
praying for you sinners,
now and at the hour of your death.

Our Lady of 'No Regerts'

Our Lady of No Regerts, prevention of bad tattoos
must be your side hustle, a part-time ministry,
because, queen of inky heaven, with respect,

a few too many permanent atrocities
have escaped your intervention. Just when it seems
the world of ink has collected its wits,

another troll with armpit hair is born,
or a Patrick Swayze centaur in a rainbow breeze.
So many RIPs, so many mama's boys, so many

portraits of you, with liberties—from the reverent,
to the sexy-but-still-chaste, to Dia de los Muertos Mary,
rainbow kewpie with a fleshed-out skull, gown

lifted to reveal pistols inked on juicy, half-spread thighs.
Are you angry to have been made kittenish,
sweet lady? What's better—to be forgotten,

or to mingle on the flash art wall among vixens
with spade-tipped tails? Mother to so many
bad-inked guys and dolls, how do you stay calm?

My mother wept over my tattoo, a fish
in multi-color flames swimming up my back.
Bad ink claims Nothing last's forever,

except, of course, YOLO spelled in penises,
a jigsaw puzzle face, and SORRY MOM
stamped across the knuckles of two fists.

But what about a mother's grief over children
delivered with no guarantees? They are born,
they whine, they steal change from your purse,

they pierce their ears and brand themselves with ice.
No blank space, anymore, on their baby skin, to mark
with kisses. Just scribbles. Other people's names inside of hearts.

Mary Has Left the Building

I like those 7-day saint candles,
cheap dollar ones from the grocery.
First was Sacred Heart Jesus in sweet vanilla,
then Virgin Mary as Our Lady of Guadalupe,
in a cloying floral scented red wax,
Soon after, Saint Jude, with his pine freshness.

But then in a little funky gift shop
I found Frida Kahlo in cinnamon spice.
Soon after I added Ruth Bader Ginsberg,
Patron Saint of Justice and general bad-assery.
Anthony Bourdain, Saint of Cooking
I put in my kitchen window.
Then I bought the patron saints of music
Jagger, Bowie, Prince and Mercury.
Friends brought over new ones, saying
"I thought of you when I saw this."
I had to get a bigger display table.

One fateful day I noticed Mary
had somehow left the building,
Not the candle, but just the
image of Mary—on the candle.
There were still rays of celestial light
that holy backlighting
where she should have been.
The little cherub beneath her,
still there, but looking confused.
Mary had become an anti-apparition
conspicuous now in her absence.

Did she not like all the competition?
Did she not get along with Marilyn or Elvis?
Did she not like being one of so many icons,

couldn't compete with all the Etsy shops?
Had I not dusted her enough?
Did I put her too far back in the pack?

How does one deal with this?
A missing Mary is a pretty lame miracle.
How is persona non grata a call to faith?
Will people line up NOT to see the Virgin?
To worship at the spot Mary USED to be?
This image will get no likes on Instagram
amidst all the Rorschach tests of
burnt toast, wood grain and rust stains.

Do I fall to my knees in prayer,
allow the holy spirit to wash over me?
Or do I take this personally,
lash out, at my abandonment.
"Bitch, I never liked you anyway."

4. Don't Stop Believin'

A Confusion of Marys

With your long blonde hair and your eyes of blue
The only thing I ever got from you
Was sorrow, sorrow
—David Bowie, "Sorrow"

as if

a true portrait

sorrows known   sorrows shared

solitude

swords in shoulders

seven sorrows

seven moments of despair

venerated images

statues carried everywhere

a madonna in the window

graffiti on the wall

neon halo in the twilight

shadows in the square

a confusion of stories   ideas and myth

stone tears   moving eyes

as if   as if

everyone else is a non-believer

The Virgin Mary Appears in a Highway Underpass

Mary pops up in the strangest places,
usually as a window stain or sandwich,
but yesterday she dripped down the wall
of a Chicago underpass, brought the faithful
running with candles and offerings, blocked traffic.
I saw the pictures, couldn't see her face,
saw a giant, gaping vagina instead, just failed
my Rorschach Test, going to hell for sure.

If this is Mary, she sure gets around,
recasting herself as a Holly Golightly,
popping up where you least expect her,
causing trouble for the locals.
But why would she choose to appear
in condensation, burnt toast or ditch water runoff?
Some will say it's proof that she still dwells here,
runs like an undercurrent, manifests in the mundane.

I say, cut the parlor tricks, Mary.
If you want a little respect, come flaming
out of the sky on a thunder cloud,
ride it like a magic carpet over Middle America,
speak in a voice like Diana Rigg or Emma Thompson,
command attention instead of this sleight of hand,
a stain to be cleaned with soap and water,
so easily erased.

To the Girl Who Sees Miracles in Receding Water

It's been three days and you can still taste flood water.
Floorboards sag on front porches, halos of gnats hover

over puddled patches of ground. When you walk through
your backyard, the grass makes a strange sucking sound.

You spend the morning with the other kids picking up debris,
a rake, a bird bath, cracked whiffle balls, even a dead carp

tangled in tarp torn loose from a neighbor's wood pile.
You listen as the adults take inventory of what has been found,

of what has been lost. Your mother misses her lawn ornament,
a Virgin Mary who once watched over her roses.

She thinks out loud, *It's gone for good.* But you believe in miracles,
that the boys who went camping the night before the water swelled

will be found, that government relief money will find its way here.
When you stand on the bank of the river, you could pass

as a shepherd prophet in a blue sweatshirt hoodie for veil,
wearing lipgloss that tastes faintly of Root Beer. If you look

hard enough you think you see her, cracked ceramic
lodged under a rock. Mud softens the rigid wrinkles of her veil,

darkens her fingers, her eyes, her lips so that her face burns
through water thick with a history of mill pollution

and lumberyard logs. She glows in her own dark Fatima,
a miracle for only the crayfish and brown trout.

A Stain in Florida

Her image stain appeared
on a glass office building
at the end of 1996. Mirrored panes refracting
and reflecting the silhouette of Mary.

A church moved into the space
parish on the first floor,
a rosary factory on the second floor.

Eight years later, the crowds dwindled,
the rosary factory defunct. A young man,
sophomore in high school, used
a Marksman sling shot
on the top three panes.
Mary's glittering head shattered.

Months later he turned himself in,
said the guilt ate at him, cried for hours
to the police out of regret. No parents to
punish him, he grew up in and out of foster homes.

I think of that young man; feeling
unloved and unseen, standing alone
in that parking lot at night, facing a stain
that prompted prayers and hope,
his back to the empty plastic chairs
pilgrimagers would sit in for hours.
The slingshot in his hand, stared up
at the 60 ft image, like David
to Goliath. Mary was his monster
who got the love and attention he
wanted. Raised his slingshot and
severed her head. Hoping
people would finally turn theirs
to look at him.

The Virgin Mary Sits Across from Me, Applying Mascara on a Northbound London Tube

There she is, across the stuttering canyon,
apparition as brief as a cough, deriving
long arcs of blackened curls up from her
plum-coloured eyelids into dazzling lashes.

Perhaps she just wants to ride for awhile,
applying kohl through the charcoal tunnel,
dissolving to reveal an empty seat whenever
a pregnant woman boards in rush-hour panic.

No shame in looking nice, even with nowhere
left to go, having exchanged the cedars
for dogwood, the dry Jerusalem winters
for drizzle and fluorescent overcast.

Crying only smudges, so she holds herself
together with a bourbon-watery gaze, emits
only the slow, steady notes of cat-gut,
pulled into wire, grazed by a resined bow.

She hums her cello-concerto while the tube
claws through a cabled underworld, passages
of memory as brittle as meringue: her Son
not gone, but everywhere, the empty crosses

raised in wood and stone, shadowless at noon.
But here, she can almost remember to forget,
watching her face in the black glass behind me,
penciling her lips to a crimson wound.

Encountering Mary Outside Lourdes

On the road leaving Lourdes
near the shuttered *Discothèque My Sweet Lord*,
stands another ubiquitous statue
of the Blessed Virgin Mary:
Our Lady of the Corn Stalks,
I'm calling her. Nothing here
is an apparition. This is Mary
in the everyday, the ordinary,
the kind of woman who might
stop you in the parking lot
as you are leaving the local *salon de thé*,
crumbs of a croissant still on your lips,
to say your tunic *est très jolie*,
that *les couleurs sont bonnes pour vous*,
then realizing you don't speak much French,
gently runs her thumb down
the middle of your body, like a surgeon
about to do a heart bypass,
outlines your figure with both hands a bit wider
than you are, and says something
about *les boutons* as she scissors with fingers.
For a moment she stares intently into to your eyes,
waits for some kind of recognition. Not knowing
what to say or how to say it, you can only nod.
She waves as she drives away in her Citroën.
This is a woman who knows everything about alteration.

Ninja Virgin

She wraps her form in black instead of blue.
Everything's covered, shoes are flexible.
Her halo's in her backpack, zipped away.

The job is on. She climbs a block of flats.
Cuts glass using her diamond laser nails,
enters the bedroom where a sick child sleeps.
Somebody prayed? It's Ninja Virgin here.
Puts halo on. Time for a miracle.
The child turns in her sleep and starts to sweat.
Next day the doctor'll say the crisis passed.

Now Ninja Virgin's gone. She abseils down.
Crosses the busy road, picks up a dog,
that almost went beneath a taxi's wheels.
The driver sees the dog up in the air
but not the Ninja Virgin holding him.
He hits the brakes and skids but halts in time.
She's off. Another job. A homeless man
lies on the sidewalk in his tattered rags.
His head is pillowed on a bag of clothes.
A filthy blanket covers most of him.
No priest around to give him the last rites.
He sees her, smiles, says."Mary!" as he dies.
She can't save everyone. That's not her brief.
The police will find him by the morning's light.
She's closed his eyes to hide their ecstasy.

She's at the hospital. The doors swing wide.
She's only visible to those like her:
night people, loners, those who're on the edge.
The porter winks at her. She's in the ward,
unhooking oxygen, breathing her life
into the old ones fighting for each breath.

Doctors and nurses check the monitors.
A power-cut perhaps. But all is fine.
Pulses are checked. Some mini miracles,
but none acknowledged by the men of science.

It's almost morning now. She's off again
to hide her darkness from the coming light.
Her black would be no camouflage at all.
She's worked her shift. It's time for morning saints.

Pareidolia, or "If It Makes Them Pray, That's OK"

Rev. Father John Straathof, of Accra, Ghana,
regarding the image of Christ's face found in the grotto

MilknHoney was in a bad place
about to cast herself into the sea
when something brushed her foot.
Driftwood, "with the face of Jesus
starring at me." Now her life is fine
"and i wish upon whom every
is to win this will have the same
fortune I did." Starting bid, $15.
It didn't sell.

But other items have, of course—
the $28,000 grilled cheese sandwich
the offshore casino won at auction
for publicity, the sandwich nibbled,
Our Lady's face discovered, all of it
wrapped in cotton, kept in plastic. And it
never grew moldy. It brought the owner luck,
frequent wins at the casino, not to mention fame
and $28,000 on Ebay.

If I were Mother Theresa's image—I am not—
I think I really would inhabit that Dorito. If I were
Mary I would peek out of the knots of the pine ceiling
of Joey B.'s bedroom in Detroit. I would etch myself
in the stump of the hacked sumac in a crack in the overpass
in Paterson, New Jersey, in the grayest, most Spanish speaking
neighborhood, where the Superfund sites outnumber steeples, almost.

If I were the baby Jesus I might skip the Pizza Hut billboard
in Atlanta, and that Frito, though there's an argument to make
for the pierogi in Pittsburgh, with all those homesick Belarussians.
I'd get a kick out of the Cone Nebula, a fine place for watching eternity.

The Chihuahua's ear in Tennessee was perfect swaddling.
Mary gets extra credit for hiding in that sonogram
of the eight-week-four-day-old child. God bless
the human brain for the hardwiring
that sees the face everywhere.

Searching

Her nose drips
green pepper,
small mounds of moist
meat round out chin and cheeks.
Mary on meatloaf.

Her son is turning up in odd locations—
on a clean, crumpled sock in England.
In the States, he's seared himself into a stick of fish,
burnt his profile into a wedge of Texas toast.
Somewhere else, her snack-sized son is a Cheeto
curled in prayer.

She wants to lean on Joseph, tell him
this is no way to save the world
but her husband is nowhere to be found.
So Mary gathers up her congealed veil of holy
and seeps into the whorled, wooden door
of the Riddle family trailer.

She is closing in on her boy,
every grain of her being ablaze.

Annunciation

The imaginary lilystalk in the blue
   ceramic coffee–mug, with the flat
rose glazed round its side–curve
   and the last drops dry in
brown rings at the bottom, leans above the radiator (which
   repeats brazenly a running vine
on every rib), and ought—on account of its white
   weight, its bright
height—
                to topple to the floor
   causing the cup to take the tumble
too (imagine the petal–bits, the pollen grains, the blue
   shards scattered, the shatter shining about
    that dropt telegram)
            but it doesn't. It
   stays, it persists; some nearly unnoticed machinery of grace
holds it still in air. On the bed
   an open book turns its pages slowly
but the door and both the windows
   are shut tight.

Mary's Confession

I have never been to Notre-Dame.
I was not there when the fire started.
I will not be there when it is rebuilt.
I was nowhere near the Vatican
when Michelangelo carved my face,
or when a man smashed it
with a hammer.

But I have not abandoned you.
If you need me, find me in the
rustle of red leaves in gutters,
the comforting musk of dung and hay,
the startled come-cries at night.
The forests are my cathedrals—
they, too, are scarred by fire.

When you see me weeping in portraits,
my tears are for the poor and the meek,
and for the injured earth they will inherit.
Smoke rises over cities.
Holy men prey upon boys.
Children are thrown into cages.
A madman rages on this throne
with millions in his grip.
They are struggling to breathe
and there is nothing I can do.

I fled my home to save my son
but I could not protect him.
Nothing destroyed
can ever be brought back.

5. How Great Thou Art

Mary at the Louvre Confronts Her Son

Even if you begged me from beneath
the cracked paint of your body—
broken but beautiful as ever—I would not
bring you back. You are too deeply gone
and past rescue. Knowing what I know now,
I tell you, even if I had not given you
birth among the cows and dung but found you
later in a basket—a baby before it all began,
hidden in the reeds like Moses—
I would not have fished you out to fill
my emptiness, no, not even for a day.
Nor would I have called for help, consulted
a rabbi or the book. Nor would I have bent
to touch your face, humming a lullabye to calm you.
I tell you true: instead of raking my nails across
my breasts, I'd have shaded my eyes against
the sun to watch you float out to sea with all the grief
and terror unleashed upon the world in your name
still attached.

Sons

*After "Scène du massacre des Innocents,"
a painting by Léon Cogniet (1824)*

Soldiers storm the innocent
homes; pound down the doors.
Their armor clacks, swords

shear when drawn slicing
every little boy in two, some still
clutching his mother's breast.

Full moon flashes red on blades.
Leather sandals stomp the babies'
wails. A king has ladled blood.

A mother runs with babe in arms,
seeks refuge house to house,

in alleys, rooftop gardens.
Crouches with her son, ensconced
in corners and stonewall shadows.

She stops to breathe
another prayer. Kneels with him,
but doesn't see the rusted spikes.

She falls, her face to dirt.
His outstretched arms break
the fall; hands and feet bruise.

She muffles cries with prayer
and drops of myrrh on his lips.

Another mother hiding there
with a child of her own, helps
them up; the black-and-blue fading

darkness into solstice light;
sun hanging low in winter's sky.
The mothers cradle their sons

in the transparent stillness,
pressing them to their bosoms,
to their own hearts, listening.

      Mary guards her son who would
      also never say a word, even now

while the young Barabbas sleeps.
But a silent mother's tongue
is sometimes louder than death.

Introduction in Indigo Children
(After a Consult with a Medical Intuitive)

For K.A. Agodon

You kept making posters of women with
rose petals across their eyelids, then went blind.
I consulted a medical psychic who told me
I was an indigo child, great with promise, that
a star entered my body at birth. A blue-cloaked
Virgin Mary whirls above me in the air
like a dancing queen. Like Nelson Mandela and
Joan of Arc, I should expect both grand work and suffering.
Indigo children, like Ragdoll kittens, may or may not be
part alien, with independent natures and high IQs.
We usher in the Age of Aquarius (and here all I can picture
is the musical "Hair," you with daisies over your eyes
and around your blond locks a halo and me glowing blue
in the dark, letting the sunshine in.) Never mind my little brother
is the actual Aquarian, typically diffident, not at all
the whirling dervish. We decide spinning Mary's are better
than angels with flaming swords, an icon of music and celebration,
and hope I can, unlike Mandela and poor Jeanne, avoid prison.
We pray for epiphany, a star to light the way and stumble,
unmindful, on a path twisted, littered with mystic trouble.

Santa Maria Sopra Minerva

... the church not the woman,
except it really is about the woman ...
—Karen Head

1.

Mary's basilica on Minerva's temple,
a metamorphosis without a veil of myth.

Under the only medieval lights in Rome
the body of Saint Catherine lies.

Her head was always somewhere else,
now in Sienna, take it as you will.

She traded hearts with Christ,
the legend says, but that's a fable.

2.

And gentle Fra Angelico at rest
under the frescoes

of Filippino Lippi, whose father
thought much about the woman

not mystically perhaps
but she was in the flesh and in the room.

3.

The monuments of popes intrude,
but few object.

Two after all are Medici
only the third ungentle.

The pilgrims look for Michelangelo
and not the woman.

The golden loincloth of Christ Redeemer
shows a peculiar modesty.

Take it as radiance
of Incarnation.

By now we are accustomed
to *braghettoni*.

4.

In a fresco that time or wisdom
has begun to chip away

Aquinas introduces the Inquisitor
to Mary, the Angelic Salutation

over his head. Only Aquinas
looks for the water of grace.

Beyond the doors, Piazza della Minerva,
above us in Assumption the woman is serene.

Welsh Pietà

This Mary
has no composure.

Her nose is lumpy;
one suspects it runs,
despite the magnitude
of grief.

Not even her hands know
what pose to hold.

Blame the sculptor,
unskilled in the basics,
the rippling of cloth;

no sure-fingered Michelangelo
would strip her of grace
and leave her

puzzled and dwarfed
in that vast choreography
of thunder and angels:

her son
dead and awkward
on her knees

as some strange fish
she must clean and serve.

From the *Winged Virgin of Quito*, "The Dancing Madonna," to Bernardo de Legarda, Wood Carver

Venerated Ecuadorian sculpture (1734)

You made me sweat and weep and dance away
  my years on the surface of this earth. You
    put nothing between me and it but a snake—
  holiest of creatures because legless—who slithers
belly to belly with Mother Earth, skin-intimate.

I fling the blue shawl you gave me, swing
  my skirt, laugh faster, stomp higher, swerve
  and curve in a manner better suited to
a Hindu goddess than a Virgin Mary. But look now,

today you've carved feathers rippling
  from my scapula. Well, plume the serpent
    and wing my dancing feet! Feather my breast
and sprout a pair of pinions from my hips!

Give me wings that undulate heavier
    than a condor's, faster than a hummingbird's,
  more transparent than a cicada's, tinier
than a fairyfly's. And please, angle all these wings

in different and opposing directions, causing me to jig
  and hula, bellying my dance out of here, flying
    not straight up with the angels, but sideways
  with the dragonflies, swooping with the swallows,
flitting and staggering with the fritillaries.

Lemon Breast of the Virgin Mary

Up near the neck,
sticking out from unperforated cloth
like some new miracle,
it's shaped like a small lemon.
Young Jesus reaches for lemonade,
or bites the rind.
Mary does not seem alarmed
at her partial transformation to tree
like a common nymph.
She never seems surprised
to have given birth to an old man.
She does not even seem to notice
the encroaching cross, appearing
at the edge of the painting.
She is the essence of vegetal calm,
unlike her Roman counterparts,
so much pleading to remain a virgin from the gods.

Catholic Cemetery, Savannah

Even in October it's tropical, Spanish moss as crepe
    over Celtic crosses and beat-up Irish flags,
        their orange stripes gone pink from summer's UV.
            And there are Marys.
            Oh God, Mary after marble Mary,
downcast Madonnas, Mother of God, no eye-contact,
            the Mary over our aunt's grave
    also comforting nearby rows of soldiers' headstones
            rising the same two feet, same rounded corners.
            "A little Flanders Field," I say.
But no. My cousin who grew up here says
    these are the Parish nuns, fallen Sisters,
each with two carved names (so many *Marys!*)
    above the year she *Professed*, the year she *Died*,
            as though the decades between birth and Christ
            were but an anteroom, not yet true life.

And now I'm having a Thomas Gray moment,
    I'm walking their ranks as he did in his elegy
            assigning lives perhaps lived, perhaps not,
            a conceit my cousin allows
            only because we don't see each other that much.
"This Mary," I say, "came from that village near Limerick
    where they burned Edna O'Brien's *Country Girls*.
And Mary Catherine here never watched *Saturday Night Live*,
    but she crossed herself for days after hearing
    that Sinead child had ripped the Pope's picture.
            And didn't this Mary play a Pogues tape
late at night—the sea shanty her Mum used to sing.
Look at her dates—she likely taught Mary Flannery O'Connor!"
            I say they're buried so close it's like
            they're holding hands, but my cousin frowns.
"Only an Atlanta protestant," he says. "Could think such a thing."
            He has his own business, he's walking their rows

mumbling like Popeye, "I know you're here."
Until, "Ha! Found you!"
Sr. Mary Christiana
Professed 1938, Died 1980,
she who brought rulers down on boyhood hands,
foretold misery, swung girls by pigtails.
And as we stand in the wobbling heat
I keep it to myself,
how they're all listening down there
as one of their own gets her ass chewed out.

Giving Thanks at Seventy

Leo's wife is demented. After dinner, he plays the ukelele while Alvin's wife reflects on the story of how she was recently compelled to disown their second son. Everyone here has aged and they sing along to "Let It Be." At the bridge, Aubrey's wife interjects that McCartney was referring to his own mother, not the Virgin Mother. Doesn't mattah, replies Joseph's wife in Long Islandese, people can take it how they wanna take it. No one here whispers as everyone here is a little deaf. Two of the wives can sing beautifully and they harmonize by instinct. They proceed from memory and never find the words of wisdom lyric, always only remembering there will be an answer.

6. Like a Prayer

The Language of Prayer

She was beautiful on a hilltop
above the Red Lake River where clouds
dashed sunlight and the scent
of cherry and lilac drifted in, drifted out,
perfumes like a halo, or heaven.
Breezes textured the air and that word, *breeze*,
was palpable or like palpability—
you could cup your hands and take it.
I watched a fisherman below me
casting into the brown water,
and I imagined his fish wishes
or that he may have been trying
to get into the mind beneath the surface.
Who knows how to pray? Solicitous,
I moved to the edge of the sheltering hedge
made for Mary and squinted into the sun,
and the words of her prayer came as easily
to me as my own name, as the memory
of my grandmother in St. John's and the rosary,
that conduit to the actual way of praying,
speaking directly as though they were friends,
God, Mary, and Jesus, even the Holy Spirit,
(abstract but somehow still close)
but it was Mary I always came back to,
Mary who seemed most real, Mary I could ask
for favors, and thank. I knew thanking
was important, my grandmother
with her wild flowers, arranging them into jars,
the shrines I knew before I knew the words,
shrine, blessed, fruit of thy womb Jesus.

An Agnostic Prays the *Memorare*

To you do I come, before you I stand, sinful and sorrowful.

Night rattles with dogs sulking over banishment
under powerlines thrumming from coal. The roof

makes a sound like a maraca shaken by a bearded
doomsayer far from Omaha where I eat ice cream

as an indulgence for my dinner salad. The devils
of the present and devils of the past straighten

their ties and scoff at my collection of paraphernalia
while those teachers with chalk in their hands write

the same word fifty thousand ways: *learn*. My mother
smokes her millionth cigarette on the other side of town,

thinking grace is the musculature of a cat. Those eyes,
blue as a robe, watching soap operas. Mary knows.

Her piety beckons from a bathtub creche, from lava
rock, from concrete. She blinks in dark. Yes, I am

nostalgic for booze. A bright wind comes over us
from Canada and the pines gossip like grandmothers.

Hail Mary

Anonymous, among women, we wait, sharing a communal grief.
By tacit agreement, we exchange only furtive glances, denying
ourselves the comfort of direct eye contact.

A sterile nurse announces my name. I follow her down
a hollow hall to a stark room. I strip, lay myself bare
on the sacrificial altar.

This thin gown offers no protection against the chill
steel table. Feet in stirrups, eyes pinned to the ceiling,
a water stain contorts into the face of the Virgin Mary.

My fingers ache to count the long abandoned beads
of my first rosary. A gift for my communion, the tiny gold cross
dangling from a string of iridescent pearls.

Caressing them, I felt superior. I fell to my knees
to scoop them up when they broke. Cheap plastic
beads skittered across the linoleum floor in the First Aid

aisle of the drugstore, but Mother yanked me to my feet, "Leave
that junk" she hissed, pulling me along behind her to the checkout line.
I try to recall the prayers I used to recite, kneeling at my bed,

palms pressed tightly together, the nape of my neck glowed
beneath the heat of his gaze. Hail Mary, Mother
Mary comes to me. She disappears into the ceiling tile.

The Grace of Full Mary Hail

At our hour, Pray for us,
    our muffled whisper words
    slipping out of windows like smoke,
    our plastic love cups in black console holders
    offering bent red straws.
Come to us, Our Lady,
    Vanilla Car Freshener of Guadalupe.
    Dangle from the rearview.
    Sway at stops. I look backward with you.
    I see you on the skipping yellow lines.
Oh, Mother of Waiting,
    of family trips unfinished—
    Stop with us in yellow diners,
    Anoint us with griddle grease,
    Raise us up with plastic forks!
Steel is the blessed womb from which we rise,
    standing to kneel at your feet
    heading home past curfew
    to Our Lady of Perpetual Waiting.

Fire is an Event, Not a Thing

At seven, I was afraid of fire. A red engine arrived in September. The fireman taught us to stop, drop, and roll. He let me wear his hat, showed pictures of burnt curtains and broken windows, movies of houses burning. Outside a family stood in the shadows of flames. He let me pet his Dalmatian. I closed my eyes, shook my head, thought of campfire marshmallows, the old wood stove in December.

An old woman offers a coin and says everything has two faces.

That night I taught my sister to stop, drop, and roll. I held onto my safety blanket, ready to smother flames down. I shivered when I heard the furnace light. I watched the flames rise. In dreams I ran from bonfires, burning trees rolled backward.

Encyclopedia Britannica states that earth is the only planet where fire can burn.

I feared ashes that surged in winter. I shook my tooth loose. I thought of play yard slides. Afraid at five, I stood alone and watched kids giggle down. At six, I joined in and slid to the ground.

I try to light a match without trembling, pray for candles and quiet hands.

In May my fire prayers were answered. I walked to the altar, took the candle to the foot of Mary, said sweet mother, *light the wick in me*, struck a match.

One small flame in the shadows of gods.

Statue of Mary

My mother's shoulders stiffened when I said
I wanted to spend my allowance at
the Catholic Gift Shop on Chenango Street, where,
nestled in glass cases crystal rosaries,
silver medals, crosses, and scapulars
were displayed. Shelves full of statuary
lined up in anti-military rows:
the cherubs, seraphs, archangels, and saints
that populate the highest heavens.
Baby Jesus in a crèche, the Infant
of Prague, The Sacred Heart, Jesus with Cross
hoisted over one shoulder, Jesus on
the Cross, the Ascended Lord in Glory,

then the mother load: three rows of statues
depicting the Blessed Mother Mary:
Our Lady of Fatima, Our Lady
of Lourdes, Our Lady of Guadalupe—
always in blue robes over white gowns or
in white robes over blue. I selected
a small choir of angels for my dresser,
an Infant of Prague in satin robes and
a tall statue of Mary for a shelf
above my bed. Her bare foot crushed the neck
of a snake winding around our planet.

Mary could defeat evil—that's what called
to me, a presence so pure her foot crushed
the serpent I'd met in the figures of
my mother and her pediatrician-
brother. They meant me harm—that much I knew—
my father was too sick with drink to see
how much danger I was in at their hands—
their hands, poking around my young body.

Where could I go for help except the divine?
The first sight each morning, the last each night
before I said my prayers was that statue of
Mary looking down at me with such love
and affection, it drew tears of relief
from my child's eyes. Her love enveloped me.
When I went to college, my mother sold
for a dime the statue that saved my soul.

To My Lady of the Three Oaks

Before we even signed the mortgage
I found You at the plant nursery
spilling your benediction
at the feet of shoppers rushing by.

Almost three feet tall
You glowed in the inky train
of the water from sprinklers,
You, made of something like red clay.

Half my life I have been in Georgia
and it still surprises me
when I pass construction sites
and their machines trailing

the torn earth so orange-red
it leaves an afterglow
behind closed eyelids. I grew up
with dirt that yielded and brewed

seed into flower and fruit and mud
as dark as a winter night.

You remember all the prayers—
the prayer on the night of blood on the sheets,
the prayer on the days of no blood when I needed it,
the prayer about the riddle of the ghost mother,
the prayer of a loneliness like a lost headstone,
the prayer of the pill bottle that stayed closed.

Half a life
from there has brought me here.
To a yard in Georgia among three oaks

so like the old goddesses before You came.
As our secret I introduce You to them,
plant maidenhair ferns at Your feet.
Only my first offering of many,

to mark gratitude to a girl-god
for our having made it this far,
in laughing praise for the places
in which miracles grow.

To All Those Who Prayed for Me

It seems wrong. For years,   *Hail Mary full of grace*
maybe since the second I kissed
the Bishop's ring
on the cold steps of St John's,
I have not believed in prayer
or its God. I said a few more
after that day, most coerced
by threat or promise of penance.

Even grace I subscribed first
to the flight of a ball and the intersection
of a glove deep in the gap, then the lines
of a trout hovering in an eddy
of the Encampment river.

                                                             The Lord is with thee

Those I see who touch my arm
and say they've asked their God,
whole congregations of Baptists
or Methodists I don't know praying
for me, a candle flickering for me,
a list I'm on of those who need God's favor

                                                    Blessed art thou amongst women

I still don't believe, but I turn
no one, no prayer, no whispered
or chanted words, away. In
the midst of drought, the first rain
falls in splatters, pops the thick dust. I
don't believe prayer brought it. I don't

believe god's watching the smoke
from a votive candle with my name

on it work its way to heaven
like the mother of all emails.

> *And blessed is the fruit of thy womb, (Jesus)*

And I am, wrapped in the love
of wife and daughter.
I used to say this:

> *Holy Mary, Mother of God*
> *Pray for us sinners,*

but I didn't believe
in sin either. I believe
in songs: *Make me an angel*
that flies from Montgomery,
seems closer to prayer. I smile
and thank the faithful, thinking
it's not the first time I've crossed
or bordered on hypocrisy. I believe
in believing in something.

As the cancer goes away and my voice
returns, I tell them it must have worked,
their prayers, the woodpecker in the dead
loblolly, the red tailed hawk floating
the blue sky.

Hail Mary, Hail Della
Holy Ohio, Holy Sewannee, Oclocknee,
Aucilla, Wacissa. Mother of God.
Mother of my daughter. Mother of petroglyphs
and dolphin rising in the morning sun.

> *Now and at the hour of our death*
> *Amen*

After a Stroke, My Mother Examines a Picture of the Icon of Our Lady of Guadalupe

Lady, why is your countenance
the color of vole feet
draggling from the jaws of a cat?
What tribe of mud daubers
stung stars onto your mantle?
Who names the fumbles
that topple from your breasts?

Your counterspell blunts
the jagged crescent
of every campesino's
charmed and smoldering scythe.
Your spooled mouth waits to unfurl
the ticker tape of your vow.
In torchlight, your eyebrows
fly to heaven on thin wings of soot.
Only the moon survives
the crush of your heel.

Virgin of Guadalupe, I pray for your handshake,
I pray for your ribs, I pray for your hips,
the ones tugged dry
while expelling that bountiful head
ordained to gnaw
all the hangnails of history.

Steer me, Lady, through the lightning
that browns the mountains.
Drown the infections
that flush my cough into a gargle.
Virgin, who never burned a supper,
strip me of strangles, grizzles,

knots, of scratched jazz
skipping the shadows
out of my sleep.

Princess of the Aztecs,
thread my poncho with roses this winter
that I might adorn that tomb slab
where even cayenne would cool,
where your son's brain was looted
of its chemical salves,
and where his feet, which stretched the sea
smooth as a conga head,
refused to rest
at right angles to the ground.

Kiss me, mother of Mexico's hope—
your little mouth
is still rusty with smoke.

Mysteries of the Corn

Your priest of 20 years retires.
Then your hairdresser.

Elephants become sacred
and the circus leaves town forever.

Even the only queen you've known is blue,
wearing sapphires from her dead father.

Loss is the corn
on your door:

16 rows
800 kernels.

You finger each
like a rosary bead:

Hail Mary Mother of Yours
lost in plaques and tangles.

Glory Be to Your Father, livelihood
lost to her care.

Hail Holy Queen, watch over the teen shot near the corner
and for the other who died of (conjecture).

Our Father, remember the birch, lost to infestation,
and the road around the lake, no longer traveled.

Each year, the husk dries,
decays a bit more.

But you hang it anyway,
a totem to stubbornness.

After all, an ear to the ground is useless.
You know what's coming.

Contributor Biographies

Franklin Abbott is a psychotherapist, poet, community organizer, and musician from Atlanta. He is editor of three anthologies on men and masculinity and two collections of poems and stories, *Mortal Love* and *Pink Zinnia*. His double CD of original poems and songs is *Don't Go Back To Sleep*.

Ivy Alvarez is the author of *The Everyday English Dictionary* (London: Paekakariki Press, 2016), *Disturbance* (Wales: Seren, 2013), and *Mortal*. Her latest collection is *Diaspora: Volume L* (Paloma Press, 2019). Born in the Philippines and raised in Australia, she lived almost a decade in Wales before moving to New Zealand in 2014. www.ivyalvarez.com

P. F. Anderson is, during the day, the Emerging Technologies Informationist for the Health Sciences at the University of Michigan. At other times, she sings in the local LGBTQ choir, cooks and cans ferociously, writes poetry or boring reference books, and plots her superhero webcomic, sometimes all at the same time. She is a single mother, spoonie, origamist, and blogger. Her poetry blog is Rosefire Rising.

David-Matthew Barnes is an author, playwright, poet, and screenwriter. He writes in multiple genres, primarily young adult. He loves tacos, board games, pinball, white carnations, koalas, all things Disney, Nancy Drew, and everything written by Dorothy Parker, Tennessee Williams, Norma Fox Mazer, and Judy Blume. He is a member of D23: The Official Disney Fan Club, the Dramatists Guild of America, International Thriller Writers, the New Play Exchange, and the Society of Children's Book Writers and Illustrators. He earned an MFA in Creative Writing at Queens University of Charlotte in North Carolina. He lives in Denver.

Grace Bauer's most recent books of poems include *MEAN/TIME*, (University of New Mexico Press) and a 25th anniversary reissue of *The Women At The Well* (Stephen F. Austin State University Press)—a collection of poems about Biblical women. Other books include: *Nowhere All At Once, Beholding Eye*, and *Retreats & Recognitions*. She also co-edited the anthology *Nasty Women Poets: An Unapologetic Anthology of Subversive Verse*.

Julie E. Bloemeke is a graduate of the Bennington Writing Seminars and was a 2019 fellow at the Virginia Center for the Creative Arts. Her first full-length poetry manuscript, *Slide to Unlock*, was published by Sibling Rivalry Press in 2020. Her poems have been widely anthologized and appeared in numerous literary journals including *Gulf Coast, Prairie Schooner, Poet Lore, Chautauqua Literary Journal, Palooka Magazine, Cortland Review* and others. A freelance writer and editor, her interviews have recently been featured in *The AWP Writer's Chronicle* and *Poetry International*. jebloemeke.com

Laure-Anne Bosselaar is the author of *The Hour Between Dog and Wolf, Small Gods of Grief*, winner of the *Isabella Gardner Prize*, and *A New Hunger*, selected as a Notable

Book by the American Library Association. Her latest book, *These Many Rooms*, it out from Four Way Books. A recipient of the Pushcart Prize, she is a member of the founding faculty of the Solstice Low Residency MFA Program. She taught at Sarah Lawrence College, University of California, and is Santa Barbara's current Poet Laureate.

Jericho Brown is author of the *The Tradition* (Copper Canyon 2019), for which he won the Pulitzer Prize and Paterson Poetry Prize. Brown's first book, *Please* (New Issues 2008), won the American Book Award. His second book, *The New Testament* (Copper Canyon 2014), won the Anisfield-Wolf Book Award. His poems have appeared in *The Bennington Review, Buzzfeed, Fence, jubilat, The New Republic, The New York Times, The New Yorker, The Paris Review, TIME magazine*, and several volumes of *The Best American Poetry*. He is the director of the Creative Writing Program and a professor at Emory University.

Brent Calderwood is a poet, essayist, and author of *The God of Longing* (Sibling Rivalry Press, 2014). His poems have appeared in journals and anthologies including *American Poetry Journal, Crab Creek Review, The Gay & Lesbian Review Worldwide*, and *The Southern Poetry Anthology*. He has received awards and fellowships from Lambda Literary Foundation, Atlanta Queer Literary Festival, San Francisco Public Library, Napa Valley Writers Conference, and Squaw Valley Community of Writers. His essays and reviews have appeared in the *Chicago-Sun Times*, the *San Francisco Examiner, OUT* magazine, and *Gathered Light: The Poetry of Joni Mitchell's Songs*. His website is brentcalderwood.net.

Rick Campbell is a poet and essayist living on Alligator Point, Florida. His latest collection of poems is *Gunshot, Peacock, Dog* (Madville Publishing). He's published five other poetry books as well as poems and essays in numerous journals including *The Georgia Review, Fourth River, Kestrel*, and *Prairie Schooner*. He's won a Pushcart Prize and an NEA Fellowship and teaches in the Sierra Nevada University MFA Program.

Michelle Castleberry is the author of *Dissecting the Angel and Other Poems*. She is a writer and social worker living in northeast Georgia. Despite growing up Baptist, she was drawn to Catholic saints, including Mary.

Ann Cefola is author of *Free Ferry* (Upper Hand Press, 2017), and *Face Painting in the Dark* (Dos Madres Press, 2014); the chapbooks *St. Agnes, Pink-Slipped* (Kattywompus Press, 2011) and *Sugaring* (Dancing Girl Press, 2007); and translations *The Hero* (Chax Press, 2018) and *Hence this cradle* (Seismicity Editions, 2007). A Witter Bynner Poetry Translation Residency recipient, she also received the Robert Penn Warren Award judged by John Ashbery. For more on Ann, see www.anncefola.com and www.annogram.blogspot.com.

Chelsea Clarey is a lecturer at Clemson University. Her scholarship covers domesticity and domestic violence, though her course syllabi are usually more cheerful than that. She lives with her wife and their rescue dogs on a one-acre microfarm in South Carolina, where the two breed endangered geese, frequent thrift stores, and bemoan the patriarchy.

Jennifer Clark's most recent poetry collection, *A Beginner's Guide to Heaven*, was released in 2019 by Unsolicited Press. Her two other collections, *Johnny Appleseed: The Slice &*

Times of John Chapman and *Necessary Clearings,* are published by Shabda Press. She lives in Kalamazoo, Michigan. Her website is jenniferclarkkzoo.com.

Catharine Clark-Sayles has just retired from her medical practice after 40 years. She recently completed her MFA in poetry and narrative medicine at Dominican University. Tebot Bach Press has published two books of her poetry—*One Breath* and *Lifeboat*. A chapbook of poems about her experiences growing up in a military family, *Brats*, was published by Finishing Line Press last September. Catharine is currently adjusting to life out of a medical office: tidying up the garden, finding places for the stacks of books (grouped by semester across her living room floor) and trying to develop a daily writing habit.

Jill Crammond is a poet/teacher/artist, dividing her time between New York's Capital District and the Adirondacks. It came as quite a surprise to her, a lapsed Methodist girl, when Mary spoke to her one New Year's Day, asking her to write the Holy Mama's true story—the one where Mary is a single mom, navigating children, dating and all the trappings of suburbia. Jill's work has been nominated for a Pushcart Prize, and can be found in *Tinderbox Poetry Journal, deLuge, Fire on Her Tongue* (Two Sylvias Press), and most recently, *Fiolet and Wing: An Anthology of Domestic Fabulist Poetry.*

C. Cleo Creech is a tobacco farm boy from rural NC, Cleo went on to take honors English at Wake Forest University, get a degree in communications, and then study studio arts at Georgia State. He was part of the Callanwolde Ceramics Program for a number of years. Cleo is past editor of the Georgia Poetry Society, helped launch the award winning book series, *Java Monkey Speaks*, and volunteered with the Atlanta Queer Lit Fest. He has been published in a number of journals and anthologies. He is currently an Art Director and commercial artist, as well as writer.

Tom Daley's poetry is forthcoming or has appeared in *North American Review, Harvard Review, Massachusetts Review, 32 Poems, Fence, Denver Quarterly, Crazyhorse, Barrow Street, Prairie Schooner, Witness, Poetry Ireland Review,* and elsewhere. He is the recipient of the Dana Award in Poetry and the Charles and Fanny Fay Wood Prize from the Academy of American Poets. FutureCycle Press published his collection of poetry, *House You Cannot Reach—Poems in the Voice of My Mother and Other Poems*, in the summer of 2015. He leads writing workshops in the Boston area and online for poets and writers working in creative prose.

Denise Duhamel's most recent book of poetry is *Scald* (Pittsburgh, 2017). Her other titles include *Blowout, Ka-Ching!, Two and Two, Queen for a Day: Selected and New Poems, The Star-Spangled Banner,* and *Kinky*. She and Maureen Seaton have co-authored four collections, the most recent of which is *CAPRICE (Collaborations: Collected, Uncollected, and New)* from Sibling Rivalry Press in 2015. And she and Julie Marie Wade co-authored *The Unrhymables: Collaborations in Prose* (Noctuary Press, 2019). She is a Distinguished University Professor in the MFA program at Florida International University in Miami.

Rupert Fike's second collection of poems, *Hello the House*, was named one of the "Books All Georgians Should Read, 2018" by The Georgia Center for the Book. It also won the

Haas Poetry Prize from Snake Nation Press. He was named Finalist as Georgia Author of the Year after the publication of his first collection, *Lotus Buffet* (Brick Road Poetry Press, 2011). His stories and poems have appeared in *The Southern Poetry Review, Scalawag Magazine, The Georgetown Review, A&U America's AIDS Magazine, The Flannery O'Connor Review, The Buddhist Poetry Review, Natural Bridge*, and others. His non-fiction, *Voices from The Farm*, examines life on a 1970s spiritual commune.

Alice Friman's seventh collection, *Blood Weather*, is out from LSU Press. Her last two are *The View from Saturn and Vinculum*, for which she won the 2012 Georgia Author of the Year Award in Poetry. Other books include *Inverted Fire* and *The Book of the Rotten Daughter*, both from BkMk, and *Zoo, Arkansas*, which won the Sheila Margaret Motton Prize from New England Poetry Club. A recipient of two Pushcart Prizes and included in the Best American Poetry, she is professor emerita of English and creative writing at the University of Indianapolis and now lives in Milledgeville, Georgia, where she was Poet-in-Residence at Georgia College.

Jeannine Hall Gailey served as the second Poet Laureate of Redmond, Washington. She's the author of five books of poetry: *Becoming the Villainess, She Returns to the Floating World, Unexplained Fevers, The Robot Scientist's Daughter*, and *Field Guide to the End of the World*, winner of the Moon City Press Book Prize and the SFPA's Elgin Award. She's also the author of *PR for Poets: A Guidebook to Publicity and Marketing*. Her work appeared or will appear in journals such as *American Poetry Review, Ploughshares*, and *Poetry*. Her web site is www.webbish6.com. Twitter and Instagram: @webbish6.

Marcene Gandolfo's poems have been published widely in literary journals, including *Poet Lore, Bellingham Review, december*, and *RHINO*. In 2014, her debut book, *Angles of Departure*, won *Foreword Reviews'* Silver Award for Poetry. She has taught writing and literature at several northern California colleges and universities.

Lara Gularte's book of poetry, *Kissing the Bee*, was published by "The Bitter Oleander Press," in 2018. Published in national and international journals and anthologies, her poetry depicting her Azorean heritage is included in *The Gávea-Brown Book of Portuguese-American Poetry*, and in *Writers of the Portuguese Diaspora in the United States and Canada*. In 2017 Gularte traveled to Cuba with a delegation of American poets and presented her poetry at the Festival Internacional de Poesia de la Habana. She is a poetry instructor for the California Arts-in-Corrections program at Folsom, and Mule Creek prisons.

Danielle Hanson is the author of *Fraying Edge of Sky* (Codhill Press Poetry Prize, 2018) and *Ambushing Water* (Brick Road Poetry Press, 2017). Her work has appeared in over 80 journals, won the Vi Gale Award from *Hubbub*, was finalist for 2018 Georgia Author of the Year Award and was nominated for several Pushcarts and Best of the Nets. She is Poetry Editor for Doubleback Books and is on the staff of *Atlanta Review*. Her poetry has been the basis for visual art included in the exhibit EVERLASTING BLOOM at the Hambidge Center Art Gallery, and Haunting the Wrong House, a puppet show at the Center for Puppetry Arts. More about her at daniellejhanson.com.

Deborah Hauser is the author of *Ennui: From the Diagnostic and Statistical Field Guide of Feminine Disorders*. Her work has appeared in *SWWIM, Bellevue Literary Review, TAB: The Journal of Poetry & Poetics*, and *Carve Magazine* and her book reviews have been published or are forthcoming in *The Kenyon Review, Prairie Schooner*, and *Tinderbox Poetry Journal*. She has taught at Stony Brook University and Suffolk County Community College. She leads a double life on Long Island where she works in the insurance industry.

Trebor Healey is the author of *A Horse Named Sorrow, Faun* and *Through It Came Bright Colors*, as well as a poetry collection, *Sweet Son of Pan* and three collections of stories—*A Perfect Scar, Eros & Dust* and the just-released *Falling*. He co-edited (with Marci Blackman) *Beyond Definition: New Writing from Gay and Lesbian San Francisco* and co-edited (with Amie Evans) *Queer & Catholic*. He is the recipient of a Lambda Literary award, two Publishing Triangle awards and a Violet Quill award, Trebor Healey He lives in Mexico City. www.treborhealey.com

Gustavo Hernandez is the author of the poetry collection *Flower, Grand, First* (Skull + Wind Press). His work has previously been published in *Impossible Archetype, Acentos Review, Assaracus: A Journal of Gay Poetry* and other publications. He was born in Jalisco, Mexico and lives in Southern California.

Mike James makes his home outside Nashville, Tennessee. He has been published in numerous magazines throughout the country in such places as *Plainsongs, Laurel Poetry Review, Birmingham Poetry Review*, and *Tar River Poetry*. His fourteen poetry collections include: *Parades* (Alien Buddha), *Jumping Drawbridges in Technicolor* (Blue Horse), *First-Hand Accounts from Made-Up Places* (Stubborn Mule), *Crows in the Jukebox* (Bottom Dog), *My Favorite Houseguest* (FutureCycle), and *Peddler's Blues* (Main Street Rag.) He has served as an associate editor of *The Kentucky Review* and as publisher of the now defunct Yellow Pepper Press. More information about him can be found on his website, mikejamespoetry.com.

Lincoln Jaques holds a Master of Creative Writing. His work has appeared most recently in *a fine line* (NZ Poetry Society), *The Blue Nib, Mayhem, Fast Fibres*, and *Shot Glass Journal*, as well as the 2018 and 2019 Poetry New Zealand Yearbooks. His Flash Fiction has been included in *Flash Frontiers*. An excerpt from a novel in progress is included in the collection *Fresh Ink 2: A Collection of Voices From Aotearoa New Zealand*. He was a finalist in the 2018 Emerging Poets. He lives in Auckland.

Julie Kane's fifth book of poems is *Mothers of Ireland* (LSU Press, 2020). A former National Poetry Series winner, Fulbright Scholar, and Louisiana Poet Laureate, she currently teaches in the low-residency MFA program at Western Colorado University. With Grace Bauer, she co-edited *Nasty Women Poets: An Unapologetic Anthology of Subversive Verse* (Lost Horse Press, 2017), and with H. L. Hix, she co-edited *Terribly in Love*, selected poems in translation by the Lithuanian poet Tautvyda Marcinkevičiūtė (Lost Horse Press, 2018).

Tina Kelley's fourth poetry collection, *Rise Wildly*, is forthcoming in 2020 from CavanKerry Press, which also published *Abloom and Awry* (2017). *Ardor* won the Jacar

Press 2017 chapbook competition. Her other books are *Precise* (Word Poetry), and *The Gospel of Galore*, winner of a 2003 Washington State Book Award. She co-authored *Almost Home: Helping Kids Move from Homelessness to Hope*, and was a reporter for *The New York Times* for a decade, sharing in a staff Pulitzer for coverage of the 9/11 attacks. Her poetry has appeared in *Poetry East, North American Review, Poetry Northwest, Prairie Schooner, The Best American Poetry*, and on the buses of Seattle.

Blake Leland has published poetry in *Epoch, The New Yorker, Commonweal, Atlanta Review, Indiana Review, Thomas Hardy Review, Canopic Jar, The Art Section, Poetry International* (online), et al. He is a Pushcart Prize nominee. In 2013, he co-authored a selection of occasional poems, *On Occasion: Four Poets, One Year.*

Janet Lowery's poems appear in *Poetry East, Greensboro Review* and elsewhere; in anthologies: *Enchantment of the Ordinary*, Mutabilis Press; *Far-Out: Poems of the 60s*, Wings Press; *Texas in Poetry, 2*, TCU Press; and *Who Are the Rich and Where Do They Live, Poetry East* (2000). Her trilogy of plays, *Traffic in Women*, called attention to human trafficking in 2006-8 and spawned a book of dramatic monologues. Her play about the opioid epidemic, *A Heroine-Free Summer*, was produced by Mildred's Umbrella in 2017. She edited *By the Light of a Neon Moon* from Madville Publishing, 2019.

Rupert Loydell is a Senior Lecturer at Falmouth University, the editor of *Stride*, and a contributing editor to *International Times*. His many poetry books include *A Confusion of Marys* (with Sarah Cave; Shearsman 2020) and *Dear Mary* (Shearsman, 2017), and he has also edited anthologies for Shearsman, Knives Forks and Spoons, and Salt. His critical writing has appeared in *Punk & Post-Punk* (which he is on the editorial board of), *Journal of Writing and Creative Practice, New Writing, English, Text, Axon, Musicology Research, Revenant, The Quint: an interdisciplinary journal from the north* and *Journal of Visual Art Practice* as well as in books about Brian Eno and *Twin Peaks*.

John C. Mannone has work appearing/forthcoming in the *North Dakota Quarterly, Adanna Literary Journal, Number One, Windhover, Poetry South, Ekphrastic Review, Inscape Literary Magazine, Baltimore Review*, and others. He won the Jean Ritchie Fellowship (2017) in Appalachian literature and served as the celebrity judge for the National Federation of State Poetry Societies (2018). He has three collections of poetry, including the forthcoming *Flux Lines* (Linnet's Wings Press, 2020). He edits poetry for *Abyss & Apex* and other speculative and literary magazines. A retired physicist, John lives between Knoxville and Chattanooga, TN. www.jcmannone.wordpress.com.

Jennifer Martelli is the author of *My Tarantella* (Bordighera Press), selected as a 2019 "Must Read" by the Massachusetts Center for the Book. Her chapbook, *After Bird* was the winner of the Grey Book Press open reading, 2016. Her work is forthcoming in *Poetry* and *The Sycamore Review* and, most recently, has appeared in *Verse Daily, The DMQ Review, The Sonora Review*, and *Iron Horse Review* (winner, Photo Finish contest). She is the recipient of the Massachusetts Cultural Council Grant in Poetry. She is co-poetry editor for *Mom Egg Review* and co-curates the Italian-American Writers Series at I AM Books in Boston.

Pablo Miguel Martínez's collection, *Brazos, Carry Me* (Kórima Press), received the 2013 PEN Southwest Book Award for Poetry. His chapbook, *Cuent@*, was published by Finishing Line Press in 2016. Martínez's work appears in *Bilingual Review/Revista bilingüe*, *Borderlands: Texas Poetry Review*, *Gay & Lesbian Review*; anthologies *Imaniman: Poets Writing in the Anzaldúan Borderlands*, *This Assignment Is So Gay*, the forthcoming *Closet Cases: Queers on What We Wear*; and elsewhere. Support from Artist Foundation of San Antonio, Alfredo Cisneros Del Moral Foundation, and National Association of Latino Arts & Culture. Martínez is a Co-Founder of CantoMundo, a national retreat-workshop for Latinx poets.

Marissa McNamara teaches English and creative writing at Georgia State University and in Georgia prisons. She is a contributing poetry editor for *The Chattahoochee Review*. Her work has appeared in several publications including the anthology *My Body My Words* and *RATTLE*, *Medical Literary Messenger*, *StorySouth*, *Muse/A*, *Memoir Magazine*, *The Cortland Review*, and *Amsterdam Quarterly*.

Linda Parsons coordinates *WordStream*, WDVX-FM's weekly reading series, with Stellasue Lee and is the reviews editor at *Pine Mountain Sand & Gravel*. She has contributed poetry to *The Georgia Review*, *Iowa Review*, *Prairie Schooner*, *Southern Poetry Review*, *The Chattahoochee Review*, *Baltimore Review*, *Shenandoah*, and Ted Kooser's syndicated column, *American Life in Poetry*, among many others. Parsons is the copy editor for *Chapter 16*, the literary website of Humanities Tennessee, and writes social justice plays for the Flying Anvil Theatre in Knoxville, Tennessee. *Candescent* is her fifth poetry collection (Iris Press, 2019).

Robert Peake is British-American poet. He writes, publishes, gives readings, and teaches throughout the UK. His newest collection is *Cyclone* (Nine Arches Press).

Alison Pelegrin is the author of four poetry collections, most recently *Waterlines* (LSU Press 2016). A previous winner of the Akron Poetry Prize, she is the recipient of fellowships from the National Endowment for the Arts and the Louisiana Division of the Arts, and her work has been recently featured or is forthcoming in *Tin House*, *Crazyhorse*, and *Poetry East*. Born and raised in New Orleans, she's been a lifelong witness to the delightful coexistence of sacred and profane in worship, art, and life.

Lee Ann Pingel lives just outside Athens in Winterville, Georgia, with her husband and a pathologically attention-seeking cat, although she prefers rats to any other house pet. She holds degrees in creative writing, political science, and religion (none of which are good choices for earning money) and owns a freelance editing business, Expert Eye Editing (www.experteyeediting.com). Her work has been published in *Motif 2: Come What May* from Motes Books and *Crossing Lines* from Main Street Rag, as well as in *Rascal*, *Rat's Ass Review*, *Pink Panther Magazine*, *Hobo Camp Review*, *The Fib Review*, *Plainsongs*, and other journals.

Fiona Pitt-Kethley is the author of more than 20 books of prose or poetry published by *Chatto*, *Abacus*, *Salt* and others. She lives in Spain.

Kyle Potvin's chapbook, *Sound Travels on Water* (Finishing Line Press), won the Jean Pedrick Chapbook Award. She is a two-time finalist for the Howard Nemerov Sonnet Award. Her poems have appeared in *Bellevue Literary Review, Crab Creek Review, Tar River Poetry, The New York Times, JAMA,* and others. She is an advisor to Frost Farm Poetry in Derry, New Hampshire, and, for the last five years, helped produce the New Hampshire Poetry Festival. Kyle lives with her husband and two sons in Southern New Hampshire.

Steven Reigns was appointed the first Poet Laureate of West Hollywood. Alongside over a dozen chapbooks, he has published the collections *Inheritance* and *Your Dead Body is My Welcome Mat.* Reigns edited *My Life is Poetry,* showcasing his students' work from the first-ever autobiographical poetry workshop for LGBT seniors. Reigns has lectured and taught writing workshops around the country to LGBT youth and people living with HIV. Currently he is touring *The Gay Rub,* an exhibition of rubbings from LGBT landmarks and is at work on a new collection of poetry. www.stevenreigns.com

JC Reilly writes poetry, fiction, CNF, and drama. Her full-length poetry collection about witchcraft, herbalism, twin sisters, and murder, *What Magick May Not Alter,* was published in 2020 by Madville Publishing. Follow her @aishatonu or read her blog at jcreilly.com.

Todd Robinson has published two books of poetry, most recently *Mass for Shut-Ins* (The Backwaters Press, 2018). His writing has appeared in such venues as *Prairie Schooner, Superstition Review, Canopic Jar, A Dozen Nothing,* and *Sugar House Review.* He has conducted community writing workshops with The Seven Doctors Project, The Naturalist School, Nebraska Warrior Writers, Nebraska Writers Collective, and, in Athlone, Ireland, with the CÚRAM center for research in medical devices. He is an Assistant Professor in the Writer's Workshop at the University of Nebraska-Omaha.

Janna Schledorn has poems in *Presence: A Journal of Catholic Poetry, Adanna Literary Journal, Revelry, Time of Singing: A Journal of Christian Poetry, Cadence,* and *Utmost Christian Writers.* She is a co-winner of the 2016 Thomas Burnett Swann Poetry Prize from the Gwendolyn Brooks Writers Association of Florida. She teaches English at Eastern Florida State College.

Donna McLaughlin Schwender's work has appeared in Grey Wolfe Publishing's *Legends,* Haunted Waters Press' *From the Depths,* Prompt and Circumstance's *Promptly,* Raging Aardvark Publishing's *Twisted Tales Anthology,* and The Poetry Box's *Poeming Pigeons Anthology.* Donna's father gave her a rosary thirty-one years ago with a note that simply said "Congratulations. You're now an official soldier of Christ." She confesses that she's never learned how to pray the Rosary, nor has she ever gone to confession.

Maureen Seaton has authored twenty-one poetry collections, both solo and collaborative, most recently, *Sweet World* (CavanKerry Press, 2019), which went on to win the Florida Book Award for poetry. Her awards include the Iowa Prize and Lambda Literary Award for *Furious Cooking,* the Audre Lorde Award for *Venus Examines Her Breast,* an NEA, and the Pushcart. A memoir, *Sex Talks to Girls* (University of Wisconsin, 2008, 2018), also garnered a "Lammy." With Denise Duhamel, she co-authored *Caprice: Collected,*

Uncollected, and New Collaborations (Sibling Rivalry Press, 2015). Seaton and Duhamel have been collaborating for over thirty years.

Robert Siek is the author of *Purpose and Devil Piss* and *We Go Seasonal*, both published by Sibling Rivalry Press. He lives in Brooklyn and works at a large publishing house in Manhattan.

Larry D. Thacker's poetry is in over 150 publications including *Spillway, Still: The Journal, Valparaiso Poetry Review, Poetry South, The Southern Poetry Anthology, The American Journal of Poetry, Illuminations Literary Magazine,* and *Appalachian Heritage.* His books include three full poetry collections, *Drifting in Awe, Grave Robber Confessional,* and *Feasts of Evasion,* two chapbooks, *Voice Hunting* and *Memory Train,* as well as the folk history, *Mountain Mysteries: The Mystic Traditions of Appalachia.* His fourth full poetry collection, *Gateless Menagerie,* is forthcoming from Unsolicited Press. His MFA in poetry and fiction is earned from West Virginia Wesleyan College. Visit his website at www.larrydthacker.com.

Richard Utz is professor and chair in the School of Literature, Media, and Communication at the Georgia Institute of Technology. His areas of specialty include Medieval English and German literature, linguistics, and culture as well as the reception of medieval culture in postmedieval times (medievalism).

Jane Varley author of a memoir, *Flood Stage and Rising;* a chapbook of poetry, *Sketches at the Naesti Bar;* and co-author of a memoir with NCAA Hall of Fame fastpitch coach Donna Newberry. She has a PhD in poetry and creative writing from the University of North Dakota and has published many poems and reviews of poetry and fiction in literary magazines. A native Iowan, she is a professor at Muskingum University in Ohio.

Megan Volpert is the author of many books on popular culture, including two Lambda Literary Award finalists, a Georgia Author of the Year finalist and an American Library Association honoree. Her newest work is Boss Broad (Sibling Rivalry Press, 2019). She has been teaching high school English in Atlanta for over a decade and was 2014 Teacher of the Year. She writes for *PopMatters* and has edited anthologies of philosophical essays on the music of Tom Petty and the television series *RuPaul's Drag Race.*

Lillo Way's chapbook, *Dubious Moon,* winner of the Hudson Valley Writers Center's *Slapering Hol Chapbook Contest,* was published in March 2018. Her poem, "Offering," is the winner of the 2018 E.E. Cummings Award. Her work has appeared, or is forthcoming, in *RHINO, Poet Lore, North American Review, New Letters, Tampa Review, Poetry East, Louisville Review,* among others. Way has received grants from the NEA, NY State Council on the Arts, and the Geraldine R. Dodge Foundation for her choreographic work involving poetry. Her poems have received Pushcart Prize nominations for the past three years.

Tyson West lives in Eastern Washington in smoke and dust on the bottom of an Ice Age flood plain. He enjoys reciting his poetry to magpies and coyotes. He has published poetry and speculative fiction in various genres in *Lovecaftiana, Shot Glass Journal, The Fib Review, Songs of Eretz, Rat's Ass Review, World Haiku Review, Cattails,* and *Failed Haiku.* He has had two poems nominated for the Pushcart Prize. He received third place in the 2nd Annual Kalanithi Contest for his rondel "Under the Bridge". He is currently the featured U.S. poet at Muse Pie Press. For more information, visit his profile at "Haiku Registry" online.

Karen Weyant's poems have appeared in *Cave Wall, Chautauqua, Crab Orchard Review, Copper Nickel, Harpur Palate, Lake Effect, New Plains Review, Poetry East, Rattle, River Styx, Slipstream, Spillway,* and *Whiskey Island.* The author of two poetry chapbooks, she is an Associate Professor of English at Jamestown Community College in Jamestown, New York. She lives in Warren, Pennsylvania.

Cassondra Windwalker earned a BA of Letters from the University of Oklahoma. She criss-crossed the country and worked in bookselling and law enforcement before resigning her post to write full-time from the coast of southern Alaska. Her short-form work has been published in numerous literary journals and art books. Her novels and full-length poetry collection can be found online and in bookstores.

Robert E. Wood teaches at Georgia Tech and received a PhD at the University of Virginia. He is the author of *Some Necessary Questions of the Play,* a study of Hamlet. His poetry has appeared in *Southern Humanities Review, South Carolina Review, Quiddity, Blue Fifth Review, NDQ, Poets and Artists,* and *Prairie Schooner.* His chapbooks, *Gorizia Notebook* and *Sleight of Hand,* were published by Finishing Line Press. WordTech published his poetry collection, *The Awkward Poses of Others,* which was awarded Author of the Year in Poetry by the Georgia Writers Association. His latest chapbook, *Alms for Oblivion,* remembers things past.

Editor Biographies

KAREN HEAD is the author of *Disrupt This!: MOOCs and the Promises of Technology* (a nonfiction book about issues in contemporary higher education), as well as four books of poetry (*Sassing, My Paris Year, Shadow Boxes* and *On Occasion: Four Poets, One Year*). She also co-edited the poetry anthology *Teaching as a Human Experience: An Anthology of Poetry*, and has exhibited several acclaimed digital poetry projects, including her project "Monumental" (part of Antony Gormley's *One and Other Project*) which was detailed in a *TIME* online mini-documentary. Her poetry appears in many national and international journals and anthologies. In 2010 she won the Oxford International Women's Festival Poetry Prize. She serves as Editor of the international poetry journal *Atlanta Review* and as secretary for the Poetry Atlanta Board of Directors. On a more unusual note, she is currently the Poet Laureate of Waffle House—a title that reflects her outreach program to bring arts awareness to rural high schools in Georgia, generously sponsored by the Waffle House Foundation. She is an Associate Professor in the School of Literature, Media, and Communication at the Georgia Institute of Technology, where she also serves as the Executive Director of the Naugle Communication Center. For seventeen years, Head has been a visiting artist and scholar at the Institute for American Studies at Technische Universität Dortmund in Germany.

Currently a member of the Atlanta Friends Meeting (Quakers), she was, for many years, a practicing Catholic. She still prays the rosary and thinks that the Blessed Virgin Mother is one of the most badass women in history.

COLLIN KELLEY is the author of the poetry collections *Midnight in a Perfect World* (Sibling Rivalry Press), *Better To Travel* (Poetry Atlanta Press), *Slow To Burn* (Seven Kitchens Press), and *Render* (Sibling Rivalry Press), chosen by the American Library Association for its 2014 Over the Rainbow Book List and as one of the best books of the year by the Atlanta Journal-Constitution. He is also the author of The Venus Trilogy of novels—*Conquering Venus, Remain In Light* and *Leaving Paris*—also published by Sibling Rivalry Press. *Remain In Light* was the runner-up for the 2013 Georgia Author of the Year Award in Fiction and a 2012 finalist for the Townsend Prize for Fiction. Kelley is also the author of the short story collection, *Kiss Shot* (Amazon Kindle Exclusive). A recipient of the Georgia Author of the Year Award and Deep South Festival of Writers Award, Kelley's poetry, reviews, essays and interviews have appeared in magazines, journals and anthologies around the world. Visit him at www.collinkelley.com.

CPSIA information can be obtained
at www.ICGtesting.com
Printed in the USA
LVHW111321181120
672034LV00026B/260

9 781948 692427